C R E A T E   Y O U R   R E T I R E M E N T

55 Ways to Empower the Rest of Your Life

Order this book online at www.trafford.com
or email orders@trafford.com

Most Trafford titles are also available at major online book retailers.

Printed in the United States of America.

Walker, Barbara M., 1935-
    Create your retirement : 55 valuable ways to empower the rest of your life /
Barbara M. Walker.
Includes bibliographical references and index.

ISBN: 978-1-5536-9814-2 (sc)
ISBN: 978-1-4122-4963-8 (e)

    1. Retirement--Psychological aspects. 2. Self-actualization (Psychology) I.
Title.
HQ1062.W33 2002   646.7'9   C2002-

Trafford rev. 02/13/2014

www.trafford.com
North America & international
toll-free: 1 888 232 4444 (USA & Canada)
fax: 812 355 4082

TESTIMONIALS

I love the way you lead the reader through the book with powerful questions and real-life examples.

Rich Fettke, MCC, Past-President of the Professional and Personal Coaches Association and Author of *Extreme Success.*

Barbara's book gave me an entirely new, exciting, positive perspective on retirement. That alone made it worth the investment of money and time.

Irene Leonard, Professional Development Coach and Lawyer. Author of *Creating the Practice You Want: A Law Practice Development Workbook.*

We do such a disservice in our culture to our retirees. They are a valuable resource to be cherished and appreciated. Barbara's book shows us all how important and possible it is to remain fully active and vibrant in our latter years. A must read for all, not just retirees. For with age comes great wisdom!

Rick Tamlyn Co-active Coach, Trainer, Founder, It's All Made Up, Inc.

The Internet resources are very helpful all listed close together. Great job and every wish for success!

E.W. Truant, Published Poet.

I think the concept is excellent; it is a very exciting project.

L.R. Neaman, Entrepreneur.

This book offers valuable information not only about 'how' but 'why' to create a fulfilling lifestyle in retirement.

Talane Miedaner, Author of *Coach Yourself To Success: 101 Tips from a Personal Coach for Reaching Your Goals at Work and in Life.*

Retirement offers choice and challenges. You can travel, pursue a new career, write a book or do all three. You will discover how to create the (rest of your) life you want.

Dan Poynter, *The Self-Publishing Manual,* http://ParaPub.com.

Create Your Retirement® is the perfect solution for people approaching retirement and wondering what they'll do next, and for those already retired and asking if this is all there is. Unlike other books on retiring that focus on financial planning, Barbara Walker has written a book for the 'new retirees,' the baby boomers still young at heart, who are seeking fulfillment, value and purpose in their retirement years. Barbara's practical exercises and enthusiastic style encourage readers to expand their traditional thinking about retirement to discover a new path, implement changes, and create a plan for the rest of their lives.

C.J. Hayden, MCC, Author of *Get Clients Now!*

Biography

Barbara M. Walker, M Ed, MBA, CPCC

Barbara is the Retirement Lifestyle Coach who uses her skills, knowledge and experience to inspire executives and professionals to create their own unique retirement lifestyle.

She is an experienced life coach certified by the Coaches Training Institute of San Rafael, California (CTI). As a professional coach, Barbara is a member of the International Coach Federation (ICF).

In addition to being an executive officer for many years, Barbara holds degrees in music, education and international business management. Now, as writer and speaker on the topic of living a successful and fulfilling lifestyle in retirement, she uses her connection to music, nature, beauty and the sacred to create powerful breakthroughs with individuals and groups.

Barbara M. Walker can be reached at:

barbara@bmwalker.com
www.bmwalker.com

FOREWORD

In this fast moving world, two rapidly evolving concepts are retirement and life coaching. Retirement is becoming a new LIFESTYLE—leaving traditions and stereotypes in its wake. Life coaching is having a huge impact on people who want to find balance and fulfillment in their lives.

Barbara Walker is definitely at the forefront of both of these areas. As a certified coach, she works with clients who are making significant change in their lives. As a retired person who has already retired twice, Barbara is an example of a person who is finding ways to express her own long-forgotten dreams!

Now, Barbara has written a unique book—combining the power of coaching and applying it to the lives of those who have retired or are about to retire. The need for people to find fulfillment in their lives in their retirement years has never been greater. Barbara has merged the worlds of retirement and self-help; retirement will never be the same!

Rich Fettke, MCC, Past-President of the Professional and Personal Coaches Association and Author of *Extreme Success*.

PREFACE

Why this book? Most books on Retirement are really about Financial Planning or Estate Planning. Not this book!

This book is about creating a fulfilling life in retirement; it is a crossover book between self-help and retirement.

Create Your Retirement®: 55 Valuable Ways to Empower the Rest of Your Life entices people to set out their hidden dreams, to reveal their lost hopes and to admit their secret desires, and then to plan a life to include them!

This book encourages risk taking, honesty, and trusting yourself and others to make a fulfilling life in retirement.

This book is aimed at those already retired, and it entices the Baby Boomers who are now retiring in ever increasing numbers. These Baby Boomers have had everything, done everything and will continue to be a driving force in their retirement.

They also have a deep hunger to be fulfilled. Many of them have led fast, hectic, shallow lives and they have never explored their souls or their dreams. This book invites them to do both!

Create Your Retirement®: 55 Valuable Ways to Empower the Rest of Your Life encompasses my own experience. I have retired twice AND I am having the time of my life doing the things I've always wanted to do—following my dreams!

I know that retirement can be the most fulfilling time of life. My coaching clients have left their stereotypical thinking behind, thrown off their insecurities and fears to do great things!

They have become computer literate, published authors, public speakers and lay preachers. Some have traveled to places they had always dreamed about, others have stepped into roles with family and friends in important new ways that have given them a sense of self-worth and deep feelings of fulfillment.

Retirement is a time of living and doing exciting things; it is a time of loving and helping others, and it is about finding the 'real you' within and manifesting that in all its glory!

ACKNOWLEDGMENTS

Many people assisted me in writing and producing this book. My thanks to my Virtual Assistant, Evelyn Hackl, for editing the text and researching its publication.

I am indebted to my peer reviewers: Anne Shorthouse, Beth Truant, Heather Bolton, and Lillian Neaman. I appreciate their enthusiasm as well as their criticism and helpful suggestions.

I want to acknowledge Rick Carty, graphic designer, who designed the cover and offered valuable advice.

I extend my ongoing thanks to my professional coach, Irene Leonard, who inspires me to turn ideas into reality.

My thanks to many in the coaching and publishing fields for their support: to Rich Fettke for enthusiastically embracing the concept of the book, to C.J. Hayden who offered encouragement, to Rick Tamlyn for his insightful comments, and Talane Miedaner for her leadership. I also want to thank Dan Poynter for his helpful information, and Gordon Burgett whose knowledge of the publishing field was enlightening.

I want to thank my coaching clients, all of whom have helped me advance my ideas about growing into selfhood and creating the life you want, whoever you may be, wherever you are!

I have the greatest respect and deepest gratitude for all who helped with this project.

INTRODUCTION

The current press urges people to save for retirement, and many do. Popular books suggest that there is no enjoyment in retirement unless you are well prepared financially, and that is partly true.

But the BIG NEWS about retirement is not about financial planning or just keeping busy and enjoying your life, it is about the huge impending change in the nature of retirement itself in the decades ahead!

The people retiring now are redefining retirement. The first of the baby boomers turn 55 years old in 2002. Over the next 30 years, millions of boomers will retire. On their journey through life, the boomers have transformed every stage they have passed through. They will now lead the world in transforming the retirement stage.

At age 55 some of them will be eligible for early retirement. They will join the many who have opted for early retirement over the past decade. While this trend may slow, there will be many more people who are ready and waiting to embrace the new retirement lifestyle.

Who are these retirees? Many are public sector employees who have accumulated pension benefits over many years of service. People employed in public utilities, government services and public school educators are the most likely to retire early.

People who have worked long years in stressful jobs like teaching, nursing and firefighting want to retire as soon as they can. For many reasons, more women than men retire early. People with university degrees who have earned higher incomes are more likely to retire early.

What about those who have already retired?

Many were offered retirement as a way of downsizing corporations in the 1990's. Many of these people are disillusioned with the traditional expectations and parameters of retirement. They are tired of playing golf every day. They do not like the idea of 'riding off into the sunset,' and they are certainly not finding fulfillment sitting in rocking chairs on their front porches!

We are talking about the first generation of urban dwellers to retire. They are more likely to live near a university; they are demanding and discerning, and want all the modern conveniences from coffee shops to local libraries.

They are part of the wave of people who form a phenomenon known as global aging. In the next 30 years the population of the world's senior citizens is expected to double. These better-educated seniors are, for the most part, retiring earlier and living longer.

While this trend will tax services in many areas, it will offer one of the most profound opportunities in the world today.

What will retirement become? It is uncharted territory. It will certainly be more than being financially prepared. It will be much more than just enjoying oneself and keeping busy.

Retirement will be a personal challenge. It will be a time of working for enjoyment and it will be a time for people to fulfill those dreams they have had all their lives.

The world of work will continue to change. Employers will offer incentives to entice older workers back into the work force. Included in the incentives will be flexible part-time contract work that will allow people to create a plan that provides both monetary support and personal fulfillment in their lives.

Many retirees will start their own businesses, and using their skills, do contract work for their former companies.

It will be a time to learn new skills and to share with people in new and satisfying ways. It will be a time when people immerse themselves deeply in the community and culture in which they live. For many people it will be a time of realizing why they are on this planet. And it will be a time to live beyond intention, to embrace passion and to find and submerge oneself in a life mission.

It will be a big, important evolution in the world of retirement. People will reach out in unprecedented ways and make significant contributions to the welfare of their families, neighbors, their cities and the welfare of the world at large. It is also going to be LIFESTYLE RETIREMENT. Rather than a time to retreat and withdraw, it will be a time for people to reach out to the many possibilities that are there and to find value, purpose and fulfillment in the rest of their lives.

If you are ready to explore a fulfilling lifestyle in retirement, you have come to the right place.

Create Your Retirement® suggests 55 ways to empower the rest of your life, and each section includes exercises that will make an effective plan for your fulfilling retirement. I encourage you to think and write about your new life and to discuss the many ideas with family members and friends.

Throughout the book runs a theme that embraces the ideas of virtual and virtually. The word "virtual" is used to refer to the newly evolving world of the Internet and the limitless possibilities there, and the word "virtually," in addition to meaning almost, is used to mean literally, absolutely and totally. There is a compelling parallel between the opportunities in the virtual world and the ones available in the new lifestyle in retirement. It is here that you will find the opportunities to empower the rest of your life.

Contents

Look At What You Have To Offer—Virtually A Life!

"Imagination creates reality." (Wilhelm) Richard Wagner

Today you are retired. Congratulations! Well done! You deserve it!

Of course you do, but why does it seem so empty all of a sudden?

You have worked hard all your life. You have been a steady and reliable worker. You have paid your bills and raised your family. You have supported other members of the family, and you have played an active role in your community, and everything is just fine, or is it?

1. Release your position and status

Do you miss your work? Are you wondering what the purpose is in your life? You know you still have those skills you brought to work each day, but somehow you don't know what to do with them. Everything seems so trivial. Nothing you do seems to make a difference any longer.

Your children are grown and on their own and while you love and cherish them, they do not need the kind of day-to-day help and guidance they once did. You still help out in the community, but something seems to be missing. What is it?

You were once an executive, an airline pilot, or a surgical nurse. You loved your role, or you hated your role, but at least you had a role. You knew what to do each day; you knew what to expect from others and they knew what to expect from you.

You were part of a team that shared the excitement and immediacy of your work. You were an expert and had skills—you knew that about yourself and others knew that about you.

And now? You have lost your sense of control; you are afraid on a very deep level. There is no team; you don't belong to a skilled group. You are not at the center of action and there is no sense of excitement or immediacy about today, or tomorrow, or next week. Everything seems so trivial! This is a confusing feeling.

You are experiencing a "crisis of relevance."

Think about some of the ways you can look at your life at the present moment.

ASK YOURSELF

Are you missing your work?   Yes/No

Do you wonder what your purpose in
    life is now?   Yes/No

Do you miss the status you enjoyed?   Yes/No

If yes, you are missing the established routine
    and stability that your working life provided.
    Take time to explore your feelings by writing or
    working with a life coach. Express your
    feelings of loss and confusion, and talk about
    what is missing in your life. You are
    experiencing a "crisis of relevance."

_____

_____

_____

_____

_____

Keep reading and working through this book.

2. Learn to let go

Let go of the importance your working role had in your life. This may seem very hard to do at first, but, remember, you, are a person and not a vice-president, a pilot, or a surgical nurse. You may have had that role, but let the importance of the title and the position go. Say "no" to being dependent on your previous status in order to feel good about yourself. Say "goodbye" to struggles with co-workers, frustration with the politics of the office, 12-and 14-hour days and the stress of endless deadlines and quotas. Let go of the old and be ready to create the new.

What do you have to offer? Virtually a life! Let's look at that for a moment. Think about all those life skills you acquired. Examine those areas in which you were trained or educated. Are you a skilled Salesperson? Plumber? Nurse? Office Manager? Make a list of the skills you developed in your specific area of work.

You have been planning and waiting for your retirement for years, and now you are going to make it the best years of your life!

You are saying "no" to the stressful day-to-day grind of work, to long hours, to punishing travel, to sleep deprivation, and to no time for self-care,

4

all of which have been a part of your daily routine for as long as you can remember.

What are you going to say "yes" to?

You are saying, "yes" to celebrating how good it feels to be able to make your own choices! You are saying "yes" to putting the struggles and frustration behind you, and to letting go of other people's expectations.

You are saying "yes" to creating a new and fulfilling life for yourself!

There are no stereotypes here! You are creating the new! Things are different now, and they are better because you choose that it be so! Step forward and savor this!

Letting go is important. Life has changed and this can be good and it can be bad.

We all know of people who have retired and who have gradually become more distant and listless. They do not seem to have a purpose in life. They may even have had counseling on lifestyle and stress management, but seem not to know what they really want to do in their retirement. These people are prime targets for health traumas such as heart attacks. We are not surprised to know they have developed a life-threatening disease and have died less than two years after retirement.

These people have not really let go. They are still the schoolteachers—but without a job, or the pilots without a plane. They have not celebrated their accomplishments. They have not worked out what they want in their retired lives, and they have not embraced a new and deeply fulfilling life.

What about you?

What are you letting go of?

What are you celebrating?

ASK YOURSELF

What was your working role?

_____

_____

_____

_____

What do you want to say "goodbye" to?

_____

_____

_____

_____

What skills do you have to offer?

_____

_____

_____

_____

What do you want to say "yes" to?

_____

_____

_____

What are you letting go of?

_____

_____

_____

_____

What are you celebrating?

_____

_____

_____

_____

3. Claim your rewards

Claim the rewards of your hard work and accomplishment. Even as you let go of the need to be dependent upon your previous position for your self-esteem, there are many positives you can claim and take forward into your new life. Claim your talents and your skills; acknowledge

8

your experience and training, say "yes" to the personal attributes that have always been your strength. Add this to your personality, creativity and enjoyment of life. Now you have a strong package to take you forward into many years of fulfilling retirement. Now celebrate the rewards you richly deserve!

For many people, being able to alter their domestic routine is a very special reward. Those who love to read late at night can sleep in the next morning without the nagging ring of the alarm clock! Those who love to travel can take advantage of last minute specials and answer the call to go at a moment's notice.

Having time to really enjoy one's hobbies is a great pleasure to many in their retirement years. Paul, for example, had always wanted to take the time to build a cellar of fine wines. For him, reading, researching the Internet, and traveling to Europe to visit wine producers and deal with wine merchants were combined around this pleasurable goal.

When Joan retired from her position as an office manager, she returned to university to pursue a long-time dream of completing her BA in history. She loves being with the young students who are full of energy and enthusiasm.

ASK YOURSELF

What are the rewards of your hard work? Make a
    list:

_____

_____

_____

_____

_____

What are your accomplishments? Make a list:

_____

_____

_____

_____

_____

What are the best parts of your personality?

_____

_____

_____

Describe how creative you are.

_____

_____

_____

What do you want to enjoy in your retirement?

_____

_____

_____

4. Explore your options

Are you thinking of a life of leisure? Do you need to work? Part-time? Do you want to work? Travel? Are there subjects you want to study?

Consider the work/non-work situation first. Your options are full-time paid work, part-time paid work, unpaid work, and self-employment. Those who want to be entrepreneurs will enjoy writing their business plans and setting out their ideas. They will find variety and flexibility in their ventures, and are probably people who are optimistic and like to take risks. Align your wishes with your needs to give yourself the support you need and the freedom you deserve to pursue your own interests.

Next, decide whether you will follow a life of leisure or whether you want to include volunteerism. Certainly doing something for others makes you feel good. It gives you a sense of purpose and helps you to develop interests and lasting friendships.

Consider whether you want to study, and if so will it be part-time, full-time, just for pleasure, and/or toward a degree.

Into this combination, think about how much you will travel. People often think that, in retirement, they will travel more than they actually want to or can afford. It also depends at what level you like to travel. Do you like to grab a backpack and go, or do you prefer a good standard of hotel and accommodation? All these decisions will impact on the life you create for yourself in retirement.

See yourself as someone who has choices, takes action, and operates from a position of inner strength. You are in control and you have many choices. Growing older is a challenge for mental, physical, spiritual and social activity. Be flexible, resilient, and open to new possibilities. You truly are "as old as you feel" and it is not too late to pursue your dream!

ASK YOURSELF

Do you want to study?   Yes/No

If yes, what subjects?

_____

_____

Do you need to work?　　　　　　　　Yes/No
　　Full Time/Part Time

Do you want to be self-employed?　　Yes/No

Do you want a life of leisure?　　　　Yes/No

Do you want to volunteer?　　　　　　Yes/No

Do you want to travel?　　　　　　　　Yes/No
　　A Lot/A Little

	YES	NO	FULL TIME	PART TIME	A LOT	A LITTLE
LEISURE						
VOLUNTEER						
STUDY						
WORK						
SELF-EMPLOYED						
TRAVEL						

Shade in the boxes and begin to see the design of the life you will create for yourself in retirement.

5. Build on your success

Build on your success and allow it to help you define the future. Write down those areas in which you feel successful in life. Then brainstorm to see how you can extend these areas into new and interesting experiences for your retirement. This process works whether you intend to lead a life of leisure, move into areas of life such as community work or further education, or work part time for yourself or others. You will create a new, satisfying lifestyle that is built upon your own personal strengths. This in turn will bring more success and fulfillment into your life.

Cheryl has always had strong interpersonal skills and enjoyed working with others. She has also always wanted to be involved in the political process. She turned her skills and her wishes into a new career in municipal politics. She is a great team worker and can really make things happen in meetings and in committee work. She is a terrific presenter and can express her views in both a small and a large forum. She has found a place for her strengths and is definitely building upon her previous success.

ASK YOURSELF

In what areas have you been successful in life?

_____

_____

_____

_____

_____

_____

How could you extend these areas of success into your new life of retirement?

_____

_____

_____

6. Examine your new criteria

I would like to give an example from my own experience. I decided very early in life that I would be a teacher. I did not really want to be a teacher, but choices were limited and I knew I did not want to be a nurse because my mother and my sister were both nurses. I thought I wanted to be a secretary, but my school counselor told my mother that I should be in the academic courses in high school and so I was. Being talented in music, it seemed logical to take my teaching degree in music, and I taught piano lessons while I was still in high school. After I graduated, I went on to finish my piano degree and to teach piano lessons where I started each day at 3 pm and ended at 8 pm and taught all day Saturday. After a few years it all seemed boring and I thought I should become a 'real' teacher and have my weekends and evenings to myself. Moving from elementary school teaching to secondary and then into district administration, I made my way up the ladder to a secondary vice principal and then a principal. The opportunity to move into independent education opened up and I served for five years as the Head of an independent school. During these years I raised two daughters. So, think of the roles I had—teacher, consultant, junior administrator, senior administrator, and CEO, as well as mother. And think of all the skills I learned in terms of management, politics, interpersonal relationships, leadership, and vision. But the time came when I wanted to turn all this into my own business. I thought about the criteria that would really work for me and I came up with four things that I must have:

- I wanted to work from home;
- I wanted to choose the people I would work with;

- I wanted to work only as much as I wanted to;
- I wanted to be truly in charge and not have to work for others.

When I thought about these criteria, I thought it would be highly unlikely that I would find a satisfying profession that would fit these criteria, and I was thrilled and delighted when I realized that the new profession of coaching fitted all my criteria, and further, it re-directs the many skills I had learned over the years into a new and exciting career.

Coaching is such an exciting area because a coach assumes that the client is creative, resourceful and whole. That is the first and primary aspect of this profession. I can work from home because the coaching is done by telephone and my clients call me once a week at a pre-arranged time. I work only with those people who want to make significant change in their lives, which is a very positive and fulfilling thing to help people to do. I work only as much as I want and I can concentrate on the people at hand and leave time for all the other things in my life that are important to me. And I am truly in charge! It is my business and I run it and make the decisions and take it in the direction I want. I love the autonomy!

So I am going to encourage you to look at your life experiences and the skills you have learned and used over the years. Then set out the criteria you want to have in place for the next stage of your life. Then create the experiences you want, and make them match your life purpose.

In my case, I knew the criteria I wanted in my new career but I laughingly wondered if there was anything that could encompass all of them. Happily, my work in coaching, writing and speaking fits these criteria perfectly!

ASK YOURSELF

What have you enjoyed about your working career? Make a list:

_____

_____

_____

_____

_____

If you could have had a career change, what would it have been?

_____

_____

_____

_____

How can you make retirement your career from heaven?

_____

_____

_____

_____

7. Transfer your skills

Transfer your skills from one area of life to another. List your professional skills, inter-personal skills and your leadership skills. Now, brainstorm how these skills can be used in other areas of your life. Transfer your technical skills from a workplace setting to an organization that requires these same skills. This will give you many ideas about how you can use the many skills you have!

In my case, I was a teacher and administrator, and I am now a coach. As a teacher, I learned classroom management techniques of holding a group together and working with one or two pupils at a time while monitoring the whole room. I learned how to plan lessons and to set out units of work over a term and a yearlong program. I learned to set assignments and examinations and how to calculate fairly the marks needed for each reporting period. I learned about writing curriculum and gathering the resources I needed to make learning meaningful for my students. And most of all I learned that people learn at their own rates in their own ways, and that my role was to encourage and motivate them to achieve the very best results they possibly could.

Many of these same skills have transferred into the coaching I am now enjoying. When I am coaching a small group I use the same management techniques. I still plan and prepare the possibilities for each coaching session. I still read and study to learn more about this new and growing profession of coaching, and I pass along the resources I find to my clients. And most satisfying of all, I work with my clients as partners on their individual agendas. I support, encourage and motivate my clients who are creative, resourceful and whole and I motivate them to be the best they can be.

So you see, those skills I learned so many years ago have been transformed into a new profession offering me a new way of life and a new purpose for my life, and that is the key: having a purpose for your life! Not that of your husband, your children, or your friends—a purpose for your life!

What about the other roles you have filled in your lifetime? Consider the skills you have as a parent or family member. Think of the interpersonal skills you have of listening to others or encouraging them to find their way. Or recall your enjoyment of planning events and carrying them through.

Remember the holiday celebrations you have planned and how you made it all happen—the budget set, the gifts purchased, wrapped, the house decorated, the entertaining carried out, the meals cooked and the cleaning up completed afterwards. These are all skills that can be isolated and transferred to others activities—to community events, political events, or charity events.

ASK YOURSELF

What are your professional skills? Make a list:

_____

_____

_____

_____

What are your interpersonal skills? Make a list:

_____

_____

_____

_____

_____

What are your leadership skills? Make a list:

_____

_____

_____

_____

How can you transfer these skills into your new
   life in retirement?

_____

_____

_____

_____

8. Create new roles

Retirement is an opportunity to enjoy playing a
number of new roles. What role do you see
yourself playing? Are you a caregiver, a teacher, a
listener, or an organizer? Write out the roles you
would like to have and then think of the many

ways you can interpret each role. An organizer, for example, could organize a church bazaar, an outdoor event, a flower show, a golf tournament or a wine tasting class—the possibilities are endless! Visualize yourself in these new roles, enjoying life and leading a full and satisfying retirement!

Charles was always good in the role of mediator. He knew how to work with both management and employees to resolve issues and to strengthen the working relationship. In his retirement, he continues to fulfill this role. Even though he had doubts about whether he would have clients, his reputation and understanding of his role have provided him with high-quality clients.

He is happy in his role as mediator, and he believes that if you are happy, you will attract positive things. He firmly believes that whatever role you choose to embrace, you can find deep satisfaction within it.

ASK YOURSELF

What roles have you enjoyed playing in your life? Make a list:

_____

_____

_____

What roles would you enjoy playing in your new
life in retirement? Make a list:

_____

_____

_____

How can you interpret these roles to make a
satisfying and fulfilling life for yourself?

_____

_____

_____

_____

9. View retirement as a career change

If you view retirement as a career change, you can make this one the career from heaven! Decide what criteria you want your new career to reflect. Do you want to work from home? Do you wish to meet new people? Study in a new field? Start a small business? How much traveling do you want to do? Are there financial considerations? Do you want to work alone or to share with others? Once you have decided the main criteria, use them to help plan what your next career is going to be. Starting something new will bring energy and excitement into your retirement years.

When Joyce retired from her position as a healthcare administrator she had some idea of what she wanted to do. She always knew that if she could have chosen another career it would be been one that included her love of cooking and entertaining. After doing the basic research and taking a course in managing her own business, Joyce opened her own catering firm. She loves the creative aspects of cooking new and delicious foods; she enjoys her customers as much as they appreciate her attractive table settings and unique decorations, and she loves having her own business. This is quite a career change indeed!

ASK YOURSELF

Consider the important criteria for you to have in your new life:

Do you want to work from home?   Yes/No

Do you wish to meet new people?   Yes/No

Do you want to be alone or with others?
                              Alone/With Others

Do you want to travel?   Yes/No

Do you want to study in a new field?   Yes/No

Do you want to start a small business?   Yes/No

What other criteria do you want? Make a list:

_____

_____

_____

_____

Write a description of your new career in retirement based on your criteria.

_____

_____

_____

_____

10. Live your lost dreams

Can you remember some of the decisions in your life when there were forks in the road? Have you ever imagined what life would have been like if you had taken the other fork? Did you give up a dream at some point to accommodate the necessities of life at that time? What if you now picked up that dream and made it a reality in your retirement life? Have you lost touch with people who were really important to you at one time? Do you want to revisit them and see where this leads? We all have dreams and our retirement years are the time to recapture them!

Tony was a young boy when his parents brought him to this country, but he remembered his cousins and friends in his small village in Italy. In his retirement years, he returned to visit and talk with them. He traveled to all the places he remembered as a boy. He made audiotapes of the stories he and his friends and family recalled from early times. He has recreated his family tree and his family history in pictures and stories for his children and grandchildren and has a lively correspondence with the land and people of his childhood.

In my case, I always wanted to write, and now I am following my lost dream. When I retired last year for the second time, people would say, "I hope that you enjoy your retirement," which meant, "I hope that you enjoy doing nothing much, certainly nothing of much importance to you or anyone else." When I told them that I was opening my own business as a personal and professional coach specializing in people who are going into retirement, they were amazed! When I added that I intended to write about the process, they were disbelieving! I was not following the expected actions of a retired person—relaxing, traveling, and visiting others. I am busy doing what I want to do, and writing about it!

I know it can be done! My coaching clients are finding retirement to be the most fulfilling time of their lives. They have overcome their insecurities to become computer literate, published poets, and inspirational speakers. Some have traveled to places they had always dreamed of, and others have helped out with family and friends in important ways that have given them a new sense of self-worth and a feeling of fulfillment.

ASK YOURSELF

What decisions did you make in life when there were forks in the road?

_____

_____

_____

Have you imagined what life would have been like if you had taken the other fork?   Yes/No

If yes, what was it?

_____

_____

_____

Would you like to pick up that dream now, in
 your retirement life?   Yes/No

Have you lost touch with people who were
 important to you at one time?   Yes/No

If yes, do you want to revisit them and see where
 this leads?   Yes/No

Imagine living your lost dream. What would it be
 like?

_____

_____

_____

_____

11. Become a new person

Give yourself permission to become a new person.
How long have you worn the old persona? Have
you ever thought of recreating yourself in a totally
different image? Retirement is the perfect time to
let go of the old roles, claim your rewards, build
on your success and create not only new roles,
but create a new personality for yourself!

Think about how you want to behave differently, to dress differently, and to think differently. Examine the many perspectives around each choice you make. Decide who you want to be in your life and create yourself in that image.

The most creative and productive years, according to recent research, are ahead. People today are living longer and have better health at older ages. During the past century we have gained at least 25 extra years that is added to the middle of life. There is time to develop a whole lifestyle between the years of 50 to 75.

Isabella, a charming speech pathologist, enjoyed a successful career attached to the special services department of a large urban school district. In her dreams she always wanted to live in Britain. She and her husband traveled there each year soaking up the culture and keeping their eyes open for the perfect opportunity. One day it was before them. A picturesque and secluded castle was for sale in Wales! They lost no time in purchasing it and spent several happy years having some basic renovation work done. When she retired, they sold their city home, closed their North American affairs and moved permanently into their own castle! She writes that they have become totally different people and can hardly even remember their previous lives.

ASK YOURSELF

Have you ever thought of recreating yourself in a totally different image?　　　　　Yes/No

If yes...

How would you behave differently?

_____

_____

_____

_____

How would you dress differently?

_____

_____

_____

_____

How would you think differently?

_____

_____

_____

Write out a description of the new you that you will become in your retirement life. Be bold!

_____

_____

_____

_____

12. Do different things

Pump up your confidence and permit yourself to experiment in totally uncharacteristic ways. Accept the invitation to be the Master of Ceremonies at a friend's wedding, make the toast to the bride, or even get married yourself! Breathe new confidence into everything you undertake and not only will you thoroughly enjoy yourself, but others will enjoy the new, confident and adventurous you as well!

Kevin did it on a dare, but it seems like second nature to him now. At his 60th birthday party his cousin dared him to learn how to ride a motorcycle. Kevin thought about it and decided to take up the dare. He took a three-day course on how to ride a motorcycle and was surprised and delighted to find that he enjoyed it. He liked the feel of the wind on his face and the sense of being out in the open. One of the first places he rode on his new motorbike was over to his cousin's house to thank him for setting him up on a dare that lead to doing something very different.

ASK YOURSELF

When do you feel most confident? Make a list:

_____

_____

_____

_____

What new activities would you like to do confidently in your retirement life? Make a list:

_____

_____

_____

Look at what you have to offer—virtually a life!

What can you say to yourself to encourage you to do these different things?

_____

_____

_____

13. Empower yourself

Empower yourself and become the authentic person you have always felt you were. Embrace the full range of human emotions. Allow yourself to really "feel" what life is like. Savor each day, every moment. Communicate sincerely and listen to others carefully. Enjoy being the person you were always meant to be.

During our lifetime we are conditioned into a very narrow range of emotions, yet inside we are floating, or crying. We yearn to be our authentic selves, yet we suppress anything that is not acceptable in our established lifestyle.

Retirement is the time to break out of this narrow range of emotional response. Take yourself away on a silent retreat to a secluded place for a weekend. Listen to your heart and soul. Listen to the wind and the birds. Think carefully about what they are telling you.

Reach into the depths of your feelings. Gather your strength, your vision and your courage and set off to become the open, vibrant, fascinating creature you are meant to be!

ASK YOURSELF

When do you feel you are most true to yourself?

_____

_____

_____

_____

_____

_____

_____

Which emotions are you comfortable with?

	WITHIN YOURSELF	WITHIN OTHERS
HAPPINESS		
SADNESS		
SORROW		
LOVE		
HATRED		
HOPE		
ENTHUSIASM		
EXCITEMENT		

How do you communicate with others?

	YES	NO
SPEAKING?		
LISTENING?		
WRITING?		
TALKING?		

How can you enjoy being the person you were always meant to be?

_____

_____

_____

_____

_____

_____

_____

14. Share your new lifestyle

You now have the formula for a whole new lifestyle that can last you the rest of your life. You can let go of the old and embrace the new with a fresh sense of confidence. You are now confident about sharing your talents and views; you are now exploring new lifestyles and cultural activities. You are involved in and support community-based events, and you are enjoying sharing in all kinds of events from film festivals to choral singing. You have developed new skills and transferred old ones into your new lifestyle. You have created virtually a new person to bring to the rest of your life and to offer to the world! Enjoy!

ASK YOURSELF

What do you enjoy sharing?

Your talent for playing the piano?   Yes/No

Your ability to entertain friends?   Yes/No

What else? Make a list:

_____

_____

_____

_____

_____

What would you like others to share with you?

Cultural events/plays/theatre?   Yes/No

Sports activities?   Yes/No

What else? Make a list:

_____

_____

_____

_____

Learn To Use The Internet—
The Possibilities Are Virtually Limitless!

"Whisper of dreams and hopes to me, for these are the permanent things." James W. King

Now that you are retired, you enter a world of unlimited possibility. You have always known that it is a big world out there, and now you are faced with the choice. Are you going to let your world close in and become a comfortable cocoon where you meet the same people for coffee every day and see the same people at church every week, or are you going to do something to add more variety to your life?

If you are ready to accept some new possibilities, they are virtually limitless! Retired people are moving out into the world in fascinating and varied ways. You will be delighted that you made a move to add some variety and interest to your life.

15. Explore the Internet

Begin with a first step that will take you toward your ultimate goal. With your new confidence in place, determine the way you will use the Internet. Put aside your fears about computers. Park your eyes-glazed-over reluctance to become computer literate. The Internet has unlimited possibilities and you will find it full of excitement once you get underway.

The statistics show that 43 percent of seniors— often stereotyped as techno-phobic, say email and computers have improved their lives. You can use email to stay in touch with family and friends, exchange photos, read newspapers online, look up recipes and book reviews or search out health or travel information.

ASK YOURSELF

Think about how you want your world to be.

Are you ready to add:

Variety?   Yes/No

New possibilities?   Yes/No

Describe your feelings about the Internet:

Are you afraid of computers?   Yes/No

Are you comfortable with your skill level? Yes/No

Do you use email?   Yes/No

Do you have a fax?   Yes/No

Do you enjoy Internet research?   Yes/No

Describe the computer skill level you would like
to have.

_____

_____

_____

_____

_____

_____

16. Achieve your goals inexpensively

You can join a day class or sign up for a course at
a community center. There is little cost to this.
Your access to the Internet is free and portable.
You can go onto the Internet from any computer.
See about getting a home computer by letting
your family and friends donate their old one to
you when they upgrade. Chances are they will set
it up for you as well!

My client, Jill, had been retired for several years and she felt as though the world was passing her by. She wanted to become computer literate but was bewildered and did not know where to begin. Money was an issue for her so she could not afford to go out and buy a computer, but she was determined to learn how to use the Internet.

I challenged her to find out how she could learn what she wanted at no cost! Within one week, she found that the community center had a free teaching service, and what's more she could have free access to the Internet! She was delighted and was telling her friend about this one day when her friend said, "I have an extra computer at home that I am not using. You may have it if you wish!" A free computer, and her son-in-law set it up for her in a newly organized space in a spare bedroom. She finds that she has improved her life immeasurably by having these new skills and access to the world of the Internet.

ASK YOURSELF

In order to gain more computer skills, would you
    be willing to:

Take a one-day course?   Yes/No

Take a night course of several
    weeks' duration?   Yes/No

Take an intensive weeklong day course?   Yes/No

How could you access the Internet?

At a local library?   Yes/No

At a community center?   Yes/No

At a friend's home?   Yes/No

At a family member's home?   Yes/No

Write out how you can achieve the level of computer skills you want in your new retirement life.

_____

_____

_____

_____

_____

17. Build images of possibility

Allow yourself to think in "free float." I love gardens so what can I see on the Internet? Garden shows, catalogues, garden designs, magazines, chat lines about plants and their care, groups such as rose growers etc.

Do this in many areas of your life—every area of your health and nutrition, your home, your interests. Go out there and look at the images of possibility that are available.

The Internet can be fun. Of the 90 percent of older people online, nearly a third use email daily. They communicate with friends and family and this helps them feel that they are connected.

One of the delightful things I discovered this past holiday season is that there are programs on the Internet to help you decorate your home. I was preparing for our family dinner and found an item that offered gift tags and place cards free on the Internet. The selection was good and I had my basic place card design within a few minutes. After printing them off, touching them up with some colored inks and gluing them to a piece of gift paper, I had colorful and unique place cards —for free!

ASK YOURSELF

What topics interest you? Name five:

_____

_____

_____

_____

_____

How can you expand your topics into interesting areas to explore on the Internet?

TOPIC	POSSIBILITIES

18. Explore the opportunities

Think of the images that you want to create in your life. Go online and follow these images to the opportunities you want to create in your life. An online group could be an opportunity to learn about something that has always been of interest. A chat line is an opportunity to discuss a topic of interest to you. Make a list of the opportunities you want to explore. You will set goals for these in the next section.

Do you remember when the telephone was new and how it opened up the world and provided an opportunity to talk to others next door or around the world? Do you recall those party lines with 3 or 4 parties on one line? They were confusing and imperfect, but we had a link with our neighbors that we never had before.

Today's version of the telephone is the Internet. Be brave and start talking to your children, grandchildren, or your neighbors about what they are learning and how they are using the Internet.

Do not let yourself be daunted by technical difficulties in the beginning. The Internet has limitless possibilities and it is in its infancy, just like the days of those party lines. Look where things have gone from there! To private lines, from wall phones to desk phones to car phones to cell phones. From analog to digital phones, and now to wireless—and it won't stop there!

Even your fridge is changing! The newest ones have a computer screen, video camera and Internet connection. Eventually the fridge will be able to plan menus and order groceries online when your supplies you are running out. See it at www.electrolux.com/screen-fridge.

Almost every organization you can think of is on the Internet. New organizations are being created only on the Internet—hence the term "virtual organization." These are non-threatening organizations that are busy doing many interesting things in this world and you want to be a part of this! It is fun! You can explore, chat, or order online. You can comparison shop or look for someone to assist you in whatever way you need. So, get with it! Get onto the Internet and explore its virtually limitless possibilities!

ASK YOURSELF

Would you like to shop online?   Yes/No

Do you comparison-shop online?   Yes/No

Could you go on to a telephone bridge
line and join a group listening to a
lecture about a favorite topic of yours? Yes/No

Could you go on to the Internet and
join a chat line that is discussing a
topic of concern to you?   Yes/No

Make a list of the opportunities you want to explore:

_____

_____

_____

19. Set SMART goals

Look back at the list of possibilities you created.
Now set goals for yourself that fit into the
following categories:

S	specific
M	measurable
A	achievable
R	realistic
T	time-related

Specific goals might mean deciding which organizations you want to join, or which newsletters you wish to subscribe to.

Measurable goals are ones that you know when you have achieved them. You can cross the finished ones off your list with a colored pen.

Achievable goals are ones you can actually manage to do. Deciding to lose 50 pounds may not be achievable, but losing 10 pounds may be very achievable and make an incredible difference to how you feel about yourself.

Realistic goals are ones you can make happen. Deciding that you want to be the first person to live on Mars may be a goal, but not a very realistic one.

Time-related goals are ones you accomplish within a week, a month or a year; they have a specific timeline attached to them. Each goal should meet all of these criteria.

It is important to set out what you want to accomplish so you have a sense of growing and learning, not just drifting around out there in cyberspace forever.

ASK YOURSELF

If there is one goal you want to set <u>for yourself</u> in
   your retirement life, what is it?

Is it specific?   Yes/No

Is it too big?   Yes/No

Is it too small?   Yes/No

Is it measurable?   Yes/No

Will you know when you have achieved it? Yes/No

If yes, how?

_____

_____

Is it achievable?   Yes/No

Will you actually be able to manage
   to do it?   Yes/No

Is it realistic?   Yes/No

Can you make it happen?   Yes/No

Is it time-related?   Yes/No

By when will you have achieved your goal?

_____

_____

_____

_____

20. Access amazing information

There is so much out there in cyberspace and so many ways to relate to Internet information. Let's go back to the 'virtual organizations' for a minute. While the Internet is the only place they exist, you can join these organizations, hold office in them, access the information they produce, take part in celebrations such as 'email in days' when a celebrity answers questions sent in by the members, or the group hosts a party on a bridge line so everyone can phone in and talk to one another. You will make friends, come up with ideas and gain information for yourself and others to use. You will amaze yourself once you are online.

There is a wealth of medical information online. The Library of Health Sciences at the University of Chicago provides credible information and can direct you to other sites. Go to www.uic/edu/depts/lib/health/hw/consumer.

Home and garden sites offer endless variety from information on renovations and decorating to family gardening.

You can attend an auction at www.ca.ebay.com or access the Yellow Pages at www.yellow.ca.

You can find out how to start your own business or where to find other entrepreneurs. If you want information about food, try the daily updated site www.epicurious.com that is supported by Gourmet and Bon Appetit magazines. When you are looking for fashion information try www.vogue.com or www.sephora.com for European fashion. Access information on your mutual funds at www.fundlibrary.com or find travel information at www.resortlocator.com where you can search by state or by province.

You can access the weather at www.weather.com and get information about taking care of your car at www.carcouncil.org and research consumer goods at www.consumerreports.org.

ASK YOURSELF

Are there organizations you would like to
    join on the Internet?   Yes/No

If yes, which ones?

_____

_____

_____

Would you like to hold office in them?   Yes/No

What information do you want?

_____

_____

_____

What are some of the favorite websites you like to
visit?

_____

_____

_____

21. Embrace new contacts

You will meet people in virtual organizations. You
will get to know them as you work together to
support a cause or share a concern. You can chat
to new acquaintances on a chat line, discuss your
favorite book at a regular meeting of your virtual
Book Club. Get advice about a recipe or ask a
question of any number of experts online.

You will also be able to keep closer in touch with
your family. Regular emails make you feel as
though you are much closer to them. You can
hear about your grandson's great grade in his
Reading Test and see his picture at the same
time, or let him scan in his art work and tell you
all about it. It will be a great motivator for him to
learn to read and write and it will make you both
feel very special. Let your niece know about the

interesting new neighbor who has moved in next door to you. Sending your family free e-cards on special days will add a sense of intimacy to your life.

The Internet is a great way to research the family genealogy, and it is so easy to set up a "Cousin's Club" so that the whole family can add items of interest at any time. Another idea is to set up a bulletin board service where each member of the family can contribute items of interest from movie reviews to recipes. Look at www.insidetheweb.com

---

ASK YOURSELF

Will you:

Work with others in a virtual organization?	Yes/No
Work together to support a cause or share a concern?	Yes/No
Chat to a new acquaintance on a chat line?	Yes/No
Discuss your favorite book online at a Book Club meeting?	Yes/No

Seek advice from an expert?	Yes/No
Ask questions of experts?	Yes/No

Do you like the idea of...

Sending regular emails to family members?	Yes/No
Seeing artwork that has been scanned in?	Yes/No
Seeing pictures of family and friends on your computer?	Yes/No
Sending e-cards on special occasions?	Yes/No
Receiving e-cards on special, and not so special occasions?	Yes/No

22. Appreciate the Internet's neutrality

There is no gender bias on the Internet. Nor is there obvious ageism. People with physical disabilities have equal access as do people of every race and religious background. Money is not a barrier, nor is there any social barrier. You do not have to wait for people to approach you, nor are you waiting for the phone to ring to have some company. You can take the initiative in participating on the Internet. Do not let age, lack of education or money, or a physical disability hamper you. It is neutral territory and you have free choice.

Young university men dominated the early years of computer development, but as computers have become popular, cheaper and easier to use, women have taken to them as well. In fact, women now take to computers more enthusiastically than men.

I think there are many sociological reasons why this is so. Women do not need to leave their homes to participate. They are more safe at home, not so open to attack or terrorist activity. They are not in physically dangerous places like on the streets, in the malls, or in parking lots.

The appeal of someone serving them one-on-one is growing. They can choose from a wide variety of merchandise and see exactly what they are getting. Merchandise is delivered promptly; groceries arrive within 2 hours of ordering; there are no languid salespeople to tolerate, and they can shop whenever they wish to, 24/7.

Of course the Internet has its share of bad press. There are computer viruses and sexual predators online, and some people have trouble giving their credit card numbers online. But as we begin the 21st century nearly one half of all homes has an avid Internet user, and as the Boomers become Zoomers in their retirement years this number is only going to increase.

ASK YOURSELF

Write out how the neutrality of the Internet affects you:

No gender bias

_____

_____

_____

No ageism

_____

_____

_____

LEARN TO USE THE INTERNET—THE POSSIBILITIES ARE VIRTUALLY LIMITLESS!

Accessible by physically disabled

_____

_____

Your financial situation

_____

_____

No social barriers

_____

_____

Safe environment physically

_____

_____

Do you want to take the initiative in
   contacting others?   Yes/No

If yes, what do you want...:

   One-on-one service?   Yes/No

A variety of merchandise?   Yes/No

Prompt delivery?   Yes/No

Flexibility of shopping hours?   Yes/No

23. Enjoy life-long learning

You will enjoy the many opportunities to be a life-long learner. There are book clubs that meet online, and travel groups who prepare a journey online and then meet to travel together—and make friends and visit and share photographs later. There are special groups who raise funds to support causes like breast cancer research. Being part of these activities brings something new and interesting into your life each day. You will find companionship, new friends, soul mates, and learn about especially vital and intriguing people. You will experience the bravery, the deter-mination and the indomitable spirit of others, and at the same time, learn a lot more about yourself and the world around you.

I am sure that when you embrace the Internet you will feel as though you can reach out to the whole world. I know you will enjoy your expanded knowledge and experience, and I am sure you will be delighted that you made the decision to begin moving into the world of computers. You may in fact, feel like my client, Jill, who after she got underway with the Internet, said, "I am so much more connected now, I don't know how I lived without my computer!"

ASK YOURSELF

What opportunities do you want in life-long learning?

Book Clubs?   Yes/No

Travel Groups?   Yes/No

Social Groups?   Yes/No

Fund Raising Groups for special
   causes?   Yes/No

How else can you use the Internet to enrich your new retirement life?

---

24. Live a productive life

Good for you! You have learned new skills and found people who can help you in new and important ways. Now, put all these skills together. Take the time to research organizations. Make contact with people who can give you expert advice. Learn to communicate with friends and family. Realize that cost is not a hurdle to getting onto and enjoying the Internet. Now you can reach out to virtually the whole world. I know that you can develop a varied and more productive life on the Internet!

Norm's life was one where work was balanced by free time to go fishing and hunting, and to enjoy his favorite hobby, woodcarving. When he retired he spent more time at his computer and found several websites and experts in the area of woodcarving. He began to form a new idea that would include an online business where he could sell his woodcarvings. It was very successful and gradually grew to include selling patterns for his projects and mentoring people just beginning to learn how to carve. Not only has he expanded his knowledge about the scope of the Internet, he has created a satisfying new business for himself. He says he has never been more productive in his life!

ASK YOURSELF

Which organizations do you want to research?

_____

_____

_____

Which experts do you want to contact?

_____

_____

_____

Which people do you want to be in touch with?

_____

_____

_____

How can you lead a more productive life by using
the Internet?

_____

_____

_____

_____

_____

_____

_____

_____

_____

_____

_____

_____

Think Big—
The Virtual World Is Huge!

"Life itself is the most wonderful fairy tale." Hans
Christian Anderson

Now that you are retired, you can indulge all your
fantasies! Nothing need stand in your way. As you
increase the scope of your thoughts and actions,
you will gain a new sense of control.

How big can you think?

Probably one of the people who really thought big
was Mother Theresa. She thought about the
service needed in another culture, in another
country, and in another profession from hers! We
are not all going to be saints, but there is virtue
in letting our minds drift out onto a large cloud,
really looking, and then reflecting upon what we
see.

Perhaps it is not important to you to make more
money, but it is more important to you to have
some very worthwhile activity to be involved in
and to call your very own.

25. Hold yourself big

List the many ways you are capable. Think about your potential. Reflect upon where you would like to have influence. Decide on the one important thing you would like to achieve in your life. Then ask yourself, "and what else?" How big would you like to make it?

Janice thought about the many seniors who are shut in and cannot get out to shop for groceries. She decided to take her friend, Betty shopping once a week and help her get her groceries home and put away in the fridge and cupboards. Afterwards they enjoy a cup of tea together. This experience has made a tremendous difference in both their lives. They have become better friends and Janice knows that her efforts are really appreciated.

Margaret volunteers with the Meals-On-Wheels program that delivers hot meals to seniors around noon each day. She realizes that these shut-ins so look forward to receiving their daily hot meal, and to seeing the volunteer driver even for just a few minutes. Margaret knows that people are grateful for her service and she finds that this volunteer experience enriches her life as well.

Do you want to think bigger than that? You could begin a small business delivering things to shut-ins. There are so many things they need and cannot get out to get, such as medicines, dry cleaning, mailing letters. People would be pleased to pay a fee to have these tasks looked after and you would be making a valuable contribution to the increased pleasure of people's lives.

It is easy to see how others can bring significant change in their lives and hard to see how we can do this for ourselves. Begin now by considering how big you want to hold yourself. Talk to others about where you have always wanted to serve others. Think about working with a personal coach who will assist you in turning your thoughts into reality. There is no limit to how big you can hold yourself!

ASK YOURSELF

In what ways are you capable? Make a list:

_____

_____

_____

CREATE YOUR RETIREMENT®:
55 VALUABLE WAYS TO EMPOWER THE REST OF YOUR LIFE!

What do you think your potential is?

_____

_____

_____

_____

_____

In what areas would you like to have influence?

_____

_____

_____

_____

What is one thing you would like to achieve in your new retirement life?

_____

72

How big do you want to make it?

---

26. Hold others big

Encourage others to be the best they can be. Challenge them to take on projects you know they can manage. Support others as they search to fulfill their life's dreams. Be there as others reach to achieve their potential!

One of the joys of being a personal coach is to experience the growth and change that others make in their lives. One of my clients, Tessa, had been retired for several years when we began to work together. She was feeling stagnant and unfulfilled in her life. She had always wanted to

73

be a writer and this desire was first and foremost in her mind. Within a few months, she had attended a writer's workshop, made important contacts, become computer literate and had written several poems that were published! This experience made Tessa realize just how much she could achieve and she went on to speak about her writing, to read and recite her poetry at church and community events and to help others enjoy the same satisfaction she had come to know. For me, it was very rewarding to see how big Tessa could imagine her sphere of influence to be and to see her enter it. There is huge satisfaction in holding others big!

David made one of the most courageous spiritual journeys. He was supported and held big by two close friends in his search for his true self. David was a high-school drama teacher. A sensitive man who loved the theatre and other cultural events, David became increasingly more disillusioned and discouraged at running a large theatre program in an urban school. He went through the motions; he buried himself in his hobbies and cultural events in the evenings and on weekends. He felt he would not survive if he had to continue in his position. During this journey through the dark night of his soul, David realized that he qualified for an early retirement incentive package.

He took it and yet still languished without finding his passion. With the help of his friends, he realized that stamp collecting was his passion! He increased his involvement in it and made more contacts in the field. His friends encouraged him to open a stamp-collecting store. He is tremendously happy! He does what he loves all day! He is eternally grateful to his friends for holding him big, and encouraging him to do what he loves!

Being there for another and helping them to be their best is deeply satisfying. In a very special way you will always be a part of this person's dreams.

ASK YOURSELF

How can you encourage others to be the best they can be?

_____

_____

_____

_____

How can you challenge others to take on projects
   you know they can manage?

_____

_____

_____

How can you support others so they fulfill their
   life's dreams?

_____

_____

_____

Describe yourself holding others big.

_____

_____

27. Increase your scope

Expand your thoughts to another level of importance. Apply your actions to a larger group. Transpose your strengths to another sphere of influence. Include another group or association in your scope. Let yourself think, big, bigger, biggest or municipal, state, federal, or Canadian, North American, International.

Think of the missionary nurse, Jean, who has served as a nurse in northern India for 60 years. Her work has brought her recognition both in North America and in India. She has demonstrated tremendous willpower as she has gradually increased the scope of her thoughts and actions, and now at 91, she is returning to India to oversee the construction of a medical clinic. She plans to continue to expand the sphere of her influence even further in the years to come.

So, think it out and begin by Stepping Out Of The Box. This is what I invite my clients to do at workshops. We think, we clarify, we reveal what it is that they really want, and then, I encourage them to Step Out Of Their Box! It is exciting and people really begin to live their lives in the way they have always wanted but have either resisted, concealed, or never dared! They have a wonderful time! And find balance and fulfillment as well!

So, consider the virtual business I belong to where we regularly meet on a bridge telephone line for a teleconference and there are 100 people on the line from Canada, the USA, Great Britain, Australia, and Europe. It is great fun and mentally stimulating. So, increase the scope of your thoughts. Hold others big so they can help you manifest your ideas. Think Big—The Virtual World Is Huge!

ASK YOURSELF

Can you expand your thoughts to another level of importance?

_____

_____

_____

_____

_____

_____

Which actions can you apply to a larger group?

_____

_____

_____

Which of your strengths can you transpose to another sphere of influence?

_____

_____

_____

_____

Describe a project you would like to be associated with. (Think big, bigger, and biggest!).

_____

_____

_____

_____

28. Take control

Realize that managing time is impossible. You can only manage yourself and how you choose to use your time.

Learn to compartmentalize your life. It is like working on computer software. You open a task or project, work on it and then close it up again. This saves you from feeling overwhelmed.

Bring closure even if a project is not complete. Summarize where you are on a project, make notes about what to do next, and when you return to it, you will easily be able to pick up the project at that time.

Break your day into blocks of time following the ABC's of Time Management. **A**ction Time (A), a time to achieve goals and complete essential tasks; **B**alance Time (B), a time to plan, equalize and stabilize your day; and **C**onnection Time (C), a time for self, friends, family and personal priorities.

Make a To Do List every day. Divide the tasks into Essential (A), Necessary (B), and Keeping Things Up To Date (C). Plug these into your blocks of time above.

Keep organized. Tidy up, file things effectively, and clear off your work surface as you go.

Work on one thing at a time. Have one folder you are working on open on your desk or one dish you are preparing on the go at one time. This way you can concentrate and enjoy what you are doing.

Stay focused and create your own healthy boundaries. Return telephone calls at your convenience; read to the children when you have tidied up after dinner. Control your behavior and you control your time.

Align your use of time with your long-term goals. Each day spend time working on the important goals of your life. The immediate will always intrude. Forgive it, and return to the important.

Be thankful for the 24 hours of time you are given each day. Do your best to use it wisely and you will live a balanced and fulfilled life.

One of my clients, Goldie, learned to prioritize her time into specific areas each day. She set aside time for her writing, her fitness activities, and her own swimming coachwork. Setting boundaries on how she spent her time allowed her to achieve her goals, realize her dreams, and lead a fulfilled life. She says, "Time is my servant, not my Master!"

ASK YOURSELF

Consider using these principles in your new
retirement life. Can you use:

Compartmentalization?	Yes/No
Closure even if not complete?	Yes/No
Organization?	Yes/No
Work on one thing at a time?	Yes/No
Create your own boundaries?	Yes/No

Create a day plan using blocks of time **A**CTION
TIME (A), **B**ALANCE TIME (B), **C**ONNECTION
TIME (C).

_____

_____

_____

_____

Make a To Do List for your day:

_____

_____

_____

Think about how you can align your time with the long-term goals in your retirement life.

_____

_____

_____

29. Manifest the impossible

Let yourself imagine what you really, really want. Write it down and add all the details you can to make it as real as possible. Then, let go of it and put it out there in the universe. Then trust the universe to respond in unique and interesting ways. You will, in fact, be able to manifest whatever you want!

I want to give you some examples from my own life where I have been amazed at the power of manifesting. That process of putting the criteria out there and letting it happen!

The first was in manifesting my husband, John. I really wanted the perfect partner, and I wrote out the criteria that I wanted in this person. He had to be tall, slim, well educated, cultured, and enjoy music, travel, and the finer things in life.

These criteria brought two people with those qualities into my life within two years, and ultimately resulted in what is now John's and my 10-year marriage. This relationship has supported my career development, and we have shared great experiences in musical events, travel and professional life.

The second example was in manifesting Helen's car. My friend, Helen lost her car in an accident and the insurance company wrote it off and paid her only a fraction of the car's actual value. It had been a Mercedes in great running order and excellent condition. What could she do?

I manifest with her that she needed a car that had low mileage, was in good condition, and was being given up by a person who had taken great care of it for several years. When I told my husband, he said, "There are not many of those around!" But, within three weeks, a close friend was selling a Jaguar in great condition with low mileage, and Helen got it for $5,000! We were amazed and she had enough left over from her settlement to replace her computer as well!

So, remember the power of manifesting!

ASK YOURSELF

What is the most impossible thing that you want in your new retirement life?

_____

_____

_____

Can you write more details?

_____

_____

_____

What else about it?

_____

_____

_____

_____

Can you trust that the universe will provide this for you?   Yes/No

If yes, can you let the idea go and trust that it will happen?   Yes/No

I hope your answer is 'yes!' You will be amazed!

30. Brainstorm the possibilities

Organize support groups, family, friends, and colleagues and make your own imaginary Board of Directors. Have private and extensive discussions with each group and write down the many suggestions you receive in terms of ideas and opportunities. All these may not be practical, or even possible, but they are opportunities. Include them in your thoughts.

There may be a support group at your church. Your children and grandchildren will have fresh and ingenious ideas; friends will really see you in new situations, and colleagues can be objective where family cannot.

My friend, Diane, has her own Board of Directors and she schedules regular imaginary meetings with them. She has Bill Gates among the both alive and deceased members of her board. They have lively meetings and she comes away with many new and exciting ideas.

Do not dismiss the impractical. Include the idea in your thoughts and let it float in your mind. It may not work in itself, but it may spark another really creative idea!

Do you have a special talent that you could turn into a business? Perhaps you have a special knack of creating afternoon seminars in Community Centers with a dozen people and have them pay you for the materials and your time to help them make mounted pictures of their family or greeting cards that they can give to their family members for the holidays? These solve the problem of what to give family members and bring a very personal and special family connection from one generation to another. You could do one session for adults and another for children. Let each person bring several pictures they have selected that they want to give to other family members or friends. You will make some money and have a wonderful experience learning about these people and their families. Think of the stories you will hear! Can these be turned into the poems or the verses on the greeting cards and a whole new business? The possibilities are endless. This is what I mean about thinking big! Let your imagination soar, and try one thing and let it lead you to another. You will know if it feels right and you want to repeat, expand or change any aspect of what you do.

If you really want to go commercial, there are endless ideas about the kind of business you can go into. Look for a really good personal coach and work with her to clarify your values and set your goals and set your business out in a logical fashion. You will enjoy the exercise and be thrilled with the assistance that is available. People want to help. The banker, the accountant, the logo designer all will give you lots of help and great ideas about how to proceed. Don't be bashful! You will be amazed at what you can accomplish.

ASK YOURSELF

Make your own Board of Directors. Who would you like to have brainstorming the possibilities for your new life in retirement? Name them:

_____

_____

_____

_____

When will you meet?

_____

_____

_____

_____

Where will you meet?

_____

_____

_____

_____

Who else can you brainstorm possibilities with?

_____

_____

_____

_____

31. Decide what feels best

You will know you are on the right track by how you feel. Your body will feel right; you will see a light or feel a thud in your body. You will receive a message that tells you when you are taking a truly authentic path for yourself. Listen to your body and know how you feel. Do not be talked into anything that does not feel right. Your senses, your intuition and your reflexes all monitor your life experience and they will guide you. Trust them.

I have always had an intuitive thud that lands in my mid-section whenever I receive an intuitive message. This message could be about which pair of shoes to buy or which job to accept.

Others see a light flash in their head when they receive the same kind of messages. I have come to know that I can trust these impulses and they can, in fact, help with the decision-making process. Is it fate or the voice of the universe? I do not know, but it is real and it works.

When Nicole and her friend, Gerry thought about what would feel the best, they remembered that as teenagers they had always wanted to be movie stars! Well, life got in the way, but now that they are retired, the feeling that they wanted to be in the movies returned, and they have rekindled this dream and they are 'extras' in the movie-making business. They love it! They earn extra income; they make new friends on the set of each different movie, and they get lots of reading done while they wait for their moment on the 'golden screen!'

ASK YOURSELF

How intuitive are you? Do you...

Feel when something changes?   Yes/No

See something?   Yes/No

Hear something?   Yes/No

Anything else?

_____

_____

_____

What do you know about the intuitive messages
   you receive?

_____

_____

_____

When have you received intuitive messages in
  your life?

_____

_____

_____

_____

Can/did you trust these messages?   Yes/No

32. Make your whole life work

Decide what needs to be done to adjust your life
in all areas, including money, family relationships, friendships, recreation and fun, your work
and your physical environment.

Take the time to work out your finances. The
'Financial Planning for Retirement' area of your
library or bookstore is well stocked with good
advice. Address any family problems and make a
consistent and conscious effort to work out
lasting solutions. Nurture your friendships and
enjoy them. Allow yourself to indulge in activities
on your own—enjoy solitude for learning and
spiritual renewal, but plan to enjoy activities with

CREATE YOUR RETIREMENT®:
55 VALUABLE WAYS TO EMPOWER THE REST OF YOUR LIFE!

your friends as well. Give yourself to the work of your choice and find the pleasure in making a contribution to the world.

Finally, make your home comfortable, clean and beautiful. Organize the closets the way you want; grow plants and flowers you love to have around you, and use your beautiful things for yourself and when you have others in your home. The joy of using your china cups and saucers stimulates your sense of beauty and abundance from the time you take them out of the cupboard, drink from them, wash and dry them to when you put them away again. Allow the process of enjoyment to wash over every activity all day long. Make your whole life the way you want it, and enjoy it.

ASK YOURSELF

Where in your new retirement life do you need to make adjustments?

Money?	Yes/No
Family relationships?	Yes/No
Recreation and fun?	Yes/No
Work?	Yes/No

Physical environment (home/location/
    country)?

                                    Yes/No

Other adjustments?

_____

_____

_____

What do you need to adjust to make your whole
    life work in your retirement?

_____

_____

_____

33. Ask for what you want

Let people know how to please you. Say which
restaurant you would like to visit. Tell people
what you would like for your birthday present.
Inform people you work with about what would
please you. People really do want to please others.
You are giving pleasure to others when you allow
them to please you.

For many of us, it seems easier to give than to receive, but there is a whole mindset about giving yourself permission to receive graciously. You deserve to be treated well by your family and friends, and they do want to treat you well, so let them know who you are, how you are growing and what will feed into this growth and development. They will love being a part of your new life. Remember, you being bigger permits them to be bigger, too!

ASK YOURSELF

How can people please you? Do you tell them:

Which restaurant you would like to go to? Yes/No

What you would like for your birthday?   Yes/No

What else would please you? Make a list:

_____

_____

_____

What else do you want to ask for in your new retirement life?

_____

_____

_____

34. Champion yourself

You are unique! There has never been and never will be another person like you in this world. Write down your unique qualities. Decide how you can use these unique qualities to make a difference in the world! You can do whatever you want to! Increase the scope of your thoughts and actions! Take control! Tell yourself that you can do it! Believe you can do it! You can be your own best cheerleader!

Imagine you are standing on the sidelines of the fairway cheering yourself on as you make a crucial putt. You can cheer yourself on from outside yourself as well as from within. Find the words to champion yourself and say them out loud as you begin, continue, and complete the task you have set for yourself. Dare yourself to succeed!

ASK YOURSELF

How are you unique? List your unique qualities:

_____

_____

_____

How can you use these unique qualities to make
a difference in the world?

_____

_____

_____

How can you be your own best cheerleader in
your new retirement life?

_____

_____

_____

Relax—
Retirement Is Virtually Fun!

"Inspiration is the passionate spur of a vague desire."
James W. King, a paraphrase of Michail Vrubel

What would you say if I said to you, "Your ideas are as valuable as anyone else's?" Would it boost your self-confidence? Would it free you to do what you have wanted to do all your life? That really is how it is! You can bring joy and satisfaction into your life and the lives of others once you let go of your worries and accept your own ideas. This freedom releases you to do whatever you want to.

35. Value your ideas

I want you to consider that not only are your ideas as good as anyone else's, but that each idea has validity. The ideas you hold reflect your attitudes and influence your behavior. Holding negative ideas is very much a part of our culture, and it results in biased beliefs, prejudice and bullying actions in which there is a need to lay blame. Move your ideas into a positive atmosphere where everyone's thoughts are considered equal. While this is revolutionary, it removes anxiety, encourages tolerance, invites creativity and rewards honesty. It totally eliminates the worry of thinking you are going to be wrong. So share your ideas and accept those of others; each person's views are valuable.

When you accept that nobody gets to be wrong, you will find that you free yourself from self-doubt and your mind can remain non-judgmental. You can then really listen to other people. Even if what others say hits a jarring note with you, when you have been listening carefully, you find something in what they have said with which you agree, or something positive to which you can relate. Being able to hold a neutral space creates a win/win situation. You win because you remain positive and non-judgmental, and others win because you introduce them to new perspectives around what they have said.

But more than that, you can embrace the freedom of knowing that your ideas are as good, if not better than anyone else's. There is no need to hold back on what you think or say.

Further, this freedom of knowing that nobody gets to be wrong allows you the fun of doing what you want to do! Do you love the history, culture and architecture of your city? Do you dream about hosting tour groups or directing walking tours in your own town? Would you like to meet people and have fun talking to them while engaging in what you are passionate about? This is a dream that you can make come true!

Lillian is passionate about learning about the world even though her early years did not permit her to follow through on this love. She was determined to change this in her retirement, and is now an avid traveler, a great reader and an advocate for the historical and cultural heritage of her city. Her greatest joy is welcoming groups of tourists to her city, taking them to the interesting sights and telling them the fascinating tales of how it all came to be.

She has fun meeting people, making new friends and sharing her knowledge. In return, she is invited to visit homes and cities in many parts of the world. She loves to make 'return visits' and to be shown the sights of another part of the world. She has enriched her life and made it right for her. She has created a fulfilling, enjoyable lifestyle.

ASK YOURSELF

Is there something you have always wanted to do but thought it was wrong?   Yes/No

If yes, what is it?

_____

_____

_____

What is wrong about it? Make a list:

_____

_____

_____

What is right about it? Make a list:

_____

_____

_____

How can you embrace the idea of doing the things
   you have always wanted?

_____

_____

36. Enjoy reaching out to others

You can bring pleasure to people every day. Many people are lonely and want to make connections with others. Doing something as simple as asking, "How are you?" and actually being interested in the answer means so much to people. In spite of our world filled with TV, telephones and computers, many people yearn for a kind handshake or a smile. So reach out in simple, thoughtful ways to those you see every day.

As your confidence grows, you will naturally reach out to those who are there. You can shine whether you are working with others to set out a new exhibition at your local museum, or helping out at the gift shop. Your enjoyment of others will be evident in any activity you are undertaking, such as preparing decorations for a special fund-raising event. People will respond to your confident manner and in turn, reveal their best side to you. You cannot help but grow and benefit from the growing mutual exchange that will develop.

Bruce is a musician. His life has been dedicated to conducting choirs, composing music and performing. He loves to share with people in

making music and his enthusiasm encourages
people to come out and sing!

Bruce is also an enthusiastic fundraiser for the
arts. His special talent is setting up exhibitions
and decorating for fund-raising galas. He loves
color and space and finds joy in making a room
come alive and ready to receive its patrons. He
knows that if the décor appeals to people that
they will offer more support to the arts companies
and that he, in turn, will benefit. Bruce has found
the fun in reaching out to those who are there
and creating something enjoyable and beneficial
to many.

ASK YOURSELF

What are the ways you would enjoy reaching out
to others?

Kind greetings?   Yes/No

Warm handshake?   Yes/No

Talking quietly?   Yes/No

Helping people?   Yes/No

How else can you reach out to others? Make a
  list:

_____

_____

_____

What will you receive in return?

_____

_____

_____

37. Dismiss your mistakes

Give yourself permission to learn from and laugh
off any mistakes. Mistakes? What mistakes? They
don't exist! Whether or not you are on the
computer, your mistakes will disappear into thin
air! No one remembers that you called someone
by the wrong name, or cares if you have made a
slip, so don't let yourself agonize over it! Press on,
think of the good you are doing and of how you
want to be seen. All the rest is gone!

Within this spirit of confidence, mistakes are not something to fear. They are natural and can often lead to new and interesting ways of doing things, so don't worry about making mistakes! No one will even know how it is supposed to be in the first place, so it will not matter to him or her if things are not just as you thought they should be. Try to see it from their perspective—as if this were the way it was intended to be!

Kerry learned how to let go of her fear of making mistakes and found fun in learning. Kerry had always wanted to complete her high school diploma. When she was young, her mother's health and the demands of other children and running a home had kept Kerry from finishing her matriculation. Even after years as a loyal worker, she had not forgotten her dream to finish high school. It was the one unfinished thing in her life that she regretted. She vowed to go back to school when she retired.

What she had forgotten was the fear she felt when she had to give class presentations! It almost caused her to give up her dream! But, she went to the teacher and explained her fears, and her teacher helped her prepare for her first presentation. Her one piece of advice was, "Do not worry about mistakes. No one knows what you are going to say anyway, and the fact that you are getting up and making your presentation is already making you a hero in their eyes!" She was right! Kerry made it through the first one, and the next, and gradually she learned how to control her fears, and can now make presentations without the fear of making mistakes.

ASK YOURSELF

Are mistakes serious?   Yes/No

Necessary?   Yes/No

Helpful?   Yes/No

Fearful?   Yes/No

How can you make your mistakes help you? Make
    a list:

_____

_____

_____

_____

Can you think of a mistake that turned out to be lucky/funny/advantageous?

_____

_____

_____

38. Have confidence

Relish your confidence—in yourself and in all you do. Allow yourself to feel confident about who you are, what you do, and how you like to be seen. Permit yourself to do what you want to do. Create positive affirmations that support and sustain you throughout the day, and create beliefs around the fact that you and only you, have been selected to do what you do and to be who you are. Enjoy your unique qualities and embrace yourself intellectually, emotionally and spiritually.

Some people believe that if they criticize their every action that they will improve. In fact the opposite is true. Only by speaking positively to yourself will you gain self-esteem and confidence. It takes patience to remember to speak to and about you in a positive way. Give yourself gentle reminders of how well you are doing. Of how much you have accomplished, of how much fun you are having, and how much you enjoy being who you want to be!

Each morning as I am swimming, I have a ritual of affirmations that I have created to affirm how I look, who I am, my best qualities, my dreams, my beliefs, and all the ways that I can think of to express my gratitude for all the positive things I have in my life.

Every once in a while I will come across a saying that I incorporate into my ritual. One I have added recently was suggested to me by my coach, "My talents are God's gift to me. What I do with them is my gift to God." Repeating this gives me permission to continue with the goals and projects I have set for myself.

Saying affirmations can give you a strong inner voice and the strength and determination to do what you really want to do in your life.

ASK YOURSELF

How are you confident about:

Who you are?

_____

_____

_____

_____

What you do?

_____

_____

_____

How you like to be seen?

_____

_____

_____

What qualities are you confident about in
yourself?

Intellectual

_____

_____

_____

Emotional

_____

_____

_____

Spiritual

_____

_____

_____

Other

_____

_____

_____

39. Walk your own path

You have your own inner standards of judgment and ethics that help you make your own decisions. You do not need to look to others for permission to do or not to do anything. Nor should you allow others to control your behavior by presuming that you need to please them. No one else's expectations need to get in your way. You make your own decisions about your life, its direction, and its day-to-day details. No one else can make you arrive at a certain time or behave in a certain way. You are your own person; you walk your own path through life and it is yours to enjoy.

You do not need to be anxious about meeting the expectations of others. The only person you have to please is yourself. If you honestly feel that you could have done something better, or you wish you had changed the way you did something, put it into a self-supporting affirmation. "The next time I shall…" whatever it is you would like to change. Don't berate yourself about what you perceive to be your shortcomings, just gently and lovingly make the changes you want to make and be confident that others will respond positively to the improvement as well.

Gloria is an inspirational speaker, but it has taken several years for her to feel that she can say what she wants and express herself in her own unique way. She grew up in a family where every word and action was judged by her parents. Her life was controlled by the expectations of her parents.

As a nurse, Gloria learned to listen to people's life stories. She found inspiration in them, and she found that one person's story would help another patient find the courage they needed to regain their health.

When she retired, Gloria began to speak to groups of recovering patients. At first she was nervous, but each time she did it, she told herself that it was fine and the next time would be even better in certain specific ways. She has become an interesting and empathetic speaker. People respond to her and to the stories of strength, patience and joy that she brings. She follows her own inner voice and keeps getting better and better.

ASK YOURSELF

In what ways do you trust yourself? Make a list:

_____

_____

Are there any of other people's expectations that are getting in your way?   Yes/No

If yes, what do you want to do about this?

_____

_____

In what ways do you run your own life in retirement?

_____

_____

40. Control your life

Being in control of your own life is a special joy in retirement! Nobody need ever again judge you or your work. You might work with others, or share in a special way, but no one else gets to say whether what you do is right or wrong, too little or too much. You know within yourself when things are satisfactory, when work is complete, whether there is more that needs to be done. Do not allow anybody to impose his or her standards or requirements onto you. Your soul is yours to love and to appreciate and you must guard it jealously.

You can conceive of your own ideas, put them into practical form, and revise and change them to suit yourself. And you can enjoy the doing of them and basking in the glow of satisfaction and approval you will receive from yourself and others.

Lynn had worked as an accountant for years and she was good at what she did. Her boss, however, was a demanding and egotistical person who wanted perfection but did not say what that was, so Lynn spent years trying to second-guess how to please her boss!

In her retirement, Lynn blossomed when she did not have to report to anybody. She remade her life to suit herself. She brought sewing, music and gardening back into her life. She entertains her friends and enjoys sharing all kinds of activities with them. She is good at everything she does and she enjoys the approval of those she loves. She is mistress of her life and she loves it!

ASK YOURSELF

In what ways do you value your independence? Make a list:

_____

_____

_____

What changes do you want to make to adjust your feeling of independence? Make a list:

_____

_____

41. Send yourself positive messages

Begin the moment you waken and continue throughout the day repeating some positive thoughts. Each time you see yourself in a mirror or passing a storefront, give yourself a compliment. The human psyche is fragile and it relishes constant reassurance. Your voice inside, the internal dialogue that always goes on, needs to be trained to repeat and respond only with positive messages. Choose friends, associates, and experiences that support the positive. Avoid the group with the negative agenda, the gossips or the lobbyists with a destructive issue. Rely only on your own inner joyful self and move into your own bliss!

You are not going to turn into a Pollyanna if you bombard yourself with positive messages. You will still have your share of life's challenges, sorrow and heartaches, but it is your positive attitude that will carry you through. In each instance, you will reaffirm to yourself that you have the capability to manage this situation. You will ask yourself, "What is there for me to learn in this situation?" People will know that even when you are burdened with cares, you bring a positive note to the group and everyone will feel better after you have been there. An added benefit is the strong correlation between optimism and longevity. This was one of the motivating factors for Nancy as she rebuilt her life by surrounding herself with positive messages.

Nancy spent two long years recovering from Chronic Fatigue Syndrome. There were times when she was deeply discouraged because of the endless pain, the lack of progress, and the attitude of everyone around her that there was really nothing the matter with her and it was all in her head!

Finally, Nancy was referred to a physician who specialized in helping people recover from CFS. He put her on a special diet of rich and satisfying foods; he worked with her to develop an exercise program that suited her preferences, and he encouraged her to bombard herself with positive messages. He emphasized the need to do all of these things all of the time and to rebuild her life and strength and health from the inside out.

Nancy wrote in her journal each morning about the day she was creating for herself. She asked herself what she needed to learn that day, and who she needed to be to achieve this. Then she set out, talking positively to herself, eating and exercising the way she wanted. She rebuilt her body, her mind and her soul.

In her retirement, she works with others who are in the same situation she was in. It brings her great joy.

ASK YOURSELF

How can I fill my day with positive messages?

UPON WAKING	
EARLY MORNING	
MID-MORNING	
LATE MORNING	
LUNCH TIME	
EARLY AFTERNOON	
MID-AFTERNOON	
LATE AFTERNOON	
DINNER TIME	
EARLY EVENING	
UPON RETIRING	

42. Celebrate your life

Enjoy your body and take care of your health. As they say, "If you don't take care of your body, where are you going to live?" Enjoy your family, your friends, and the neighbors. Celebrate with others as they achieve the milestones in their lives. Plan for the kinds of celebrations you want in your life. Enjoy Nature, walk in the park and pause to watch the children flying kites on a breezy day. Every activity can bring pleasure into your life. Visit a modern art gallery with a friend, share a restaurant that specializes in food you have never tried and let others know that you are the one who is always pleasant, kind and able to see the positive side in every situation.

Eric is a retired lawyer. His working life was demanding and stressful as he fought to keep abreast of the legal world and to compete with the many brilliant minds he encountered.

Eric retains his mental and physical energy, but now he gives himself permission to enjoy life to the maximum. He thrives on wildlife adventure, and has been on an African safari, hiked the mountains of Tibet, and right now he is in Alaska driving a sled in the dogsled races! There is nothing he doesn't consider doing—and the harder and more exacting the effort the more he enjoys the challenge! For him, living life to the maximum is meeting as many physically and mentally challenging adventures as he can find!

ASK YOURSELF

Can you give yourself permission to live
    your life to the maximum?   Yes/No

If yes, can you describe what the maximum would
    be for:

Your body

_____

_____

Your health

_____

_____

_____

Your family

_____

_____

_____

Your friends

_____

_____

_____

Other areas of your life

_____

_____

_____

Where else do you need to give yourself permission to live your new retirement life to the maximum?

_____

_____

_____

43. Find what is funny

There is something humorous in nearly every situation. Laugh at yourself when you do something silly. Listen for amusing bits that add spice to life and laugh at the incongruous goings on of mankind. Laughter is good for you, and a funny comment can lighten an otherwise dreary situation.

Sometimes the funny side is really an ironic twist of fate; at other times it is giving you permission to go to a ridiculously funny movie.

As a child, Loretta was always told that she could not sing. She desperately wanted to sing, but every time she tried, her brothers would clap their hands over their ears and make fun of her. In spite of their taunting, she continued to sing along with the radio over the years. When she retired she joined a community choir. With a little coaching, she discovered that she has a lovely alto voice that blends beautifully with other singers. She finds it very amusing that the very thing about which her brothers teased her as a child is now the thing that gives her so much pleasure.

ASK YOURSELF

Can you find what is funny in a situation? Yes/No

If yes, can you:

Laugh at yourself?   Yes/No

Listen for amusing bits?   Yes/No

Laugh at the funny things people do?   Yes/No

Laugh at humorous situations?   Yes/No

Describe the funniest thing that has happened to
   you:

_____

_____

_____

What do you need to do to keep the humor in your new retirement life?

_____

_____

_____

_____

44. Enjoy your choices

You have choices at every turn, from which clothes to put on in the morning and what you will have for breakfast, to how you will spend your day and what you will accomplish. Choose something important to do each day and make it happen. Keep the busy choices in control so you can enjoy the choices that shape your life the way you want it to be.

Celebrate how good it feels to be able to make your own choices. How did you get into your present situation? Through struggles, frustration, and determination? Now you can turn all of this into positive messages that allow you to claim your life. You can now celebrate, each day, as you create your own new space that reflects your own choices. Things are different now; they are better because you choose them to be so. Step forward and take hold of your own new space; savor this space; it is your choice to be in this space, and it is the new you!

Carla retired on a small pension and a great attitude. She had been part of a natural history group for years, and now she is able to step into the space of participating fully in their activities. She goes camping, hiking, and traveling into different geographical areas to observe natural phenomena, like the desert plants in bloom.

She especially enjoys the learning opportunities open to those 55 and over where she can travel, learn, and meet new people economically through www.elderhostel.org.

Carla has made positive choices in her life that give her freedom, adventure and opportunity. She sends herself positive messages that celebrate a positive attitude, and she firmly believes that she lives a life of abundance and wealth. Her self-messages convey approval of all she is and does. She truly has found fulfillment in retirement.

ASK YOURSELF

What are the choices you *must have* in your life?
Make a list:

_____

_____

_____

_____

_____

_____

What are the choices you are willing to
compromise in your life?

_____

_____

_____

_____

How can you celebrate the choices you now make in your new retirement life?

_____

_____

_____

_____

_____

_____

_____

_____

_____

_____

_____

Make A Contribution—
It Virtually Gives Meaning To Life!

"Most of us go to our grave with our music still inside of us." anonymous

I believe that many people think that the only way to make a contribution is to do it on other people's terms, but my experience convinces me that you can make a contribution on your own terms that will be both personally satisfying and valuable to others.

Here are some thoughts about how you can make a contribution:

45. Find your passion

Make an inventory of your dreams. List all the things you want to do, to be, and to share. Do not let financial considerations, age, or lack of education stand in the way. There are ways to make these dreams come true.

What is it that makes it all worthwhile for you? Is it the satisfaction of a job well done? Is it the warmth of sharing deeply with others? Do you like the excitement of never quite knowing how things are going to turn out? Your passion can direct and inform your actions when you know that you are acting in line with your dreams and goals.

Rick is an example of someone who never lost sight of his dream—his passion. Even when he was young, poor and dedicated to getting an education, he held onto his dream. He believed that there were ways to make his dream come true.

As a young man he was always an active person and an excellent athlete. In school, at university and throughout his teaching career he enjoyed keeping physically active. His dream had always been to row. He read about rowing teams; he watched regattas and rowing meets whenever he could.

In his retirement Rick had time to look for the opportunity he had dreamed about—to join a rowing club and train as part of a team. It was hard work and he loved it! He felt the adrenaline soar when they competed and their team went to the top of their division, due in no small part to Rick's energy and enthusiasm.

Rick went even further with this passion of his! He formed a rowing division for the local university and brought in professional trainers to teach and train the young people. His passion has become a major contribution to the local community and Rick has never been happier in his life!

Your dreams and goals affect the community in which you live. When you live an authentic and purposeful life, you give others the space to do the same. You are at the time of your life when your greatest contribution is to be a passionate and inspirational leader to those around you. You have more influence and can handle more than you think. As Mother Teresa said, "I know that God will not give me anything I cannot handle. I just wish He didn't trust me so much." Trust your dreams and let them lead you to do what you know you are called to do.

ASK YOURSELF

What is it that makes it all worthwhile for you? Is it:

The satisfaction of a job well done?   Yes/No

The warmth of sharing deeply?   Yes/No

The excitement of seeing how things
    will turn out?   Yes/No

Other?

_____

_____

_____

What are your dreams? Make a list:

_____

_____

_____

How can you make them come true?

_____

_____

_____

_____

46. Help others

Each of us has things we like to do that can easily help others. These can range from shopping to running errands to offering free professional advice. Each of us needs help in one way or another, whether it is with our income tax forms or our leaky tap. Help is always appreciated and often leads to friendships and other shared activities. You can never lose by being generous with your time and your talent.

Charles always loved gardening and it was his greatest regret when he could no longer manage in his own home that he had to leave his beloved garden. Not long after he arrived at the care home, however, he was drawn outside and began to poke around in the flowerbeds. He realized that the garden needed more care than it was getting and that if it had more flowers it would bring great pleasure to a lot of people. He organized a gardening committee and they designed a plan and prepared the beds and planted and tended, and the results were spectacular! Flowers enhance the tables of the dining room—bouquets welcome visitors to the reception area and bowls of color and fragrance fill the great hall! Everyone comments on the beautiful flowers, and Charles gets a lot of well-deserved credit for following through generously on something he loves!

There are so many ideas where you can really allow yourself to think outside the box. Give a hand to different organizations. Experiment with delivering a new or different kind of service to your family, friends and community. Find personal ways to express your personality and let your heart lead the way. You will know when an idea is right. Your intuition will direct you to make the right decision about the nature of your contribution.

Do you go away in the winter and are home only at certain times of the year? There are seasonal projects that you can get involved in. You do not have to worry that if you cannot be available all the time that your contribution will not be worthwhile. Think what would fit into your yearly rhythm and plan to make a seasonal contribution. Perhaps it is a charity fundraiser that always takes place in May. They would welcome your assistance and you will know that you have made a valuable contribution in helping others. So honor your own rhythm and preferred time and be assured that your input will be valued and appreciated by the organizers and by the recipients.

ASK YOURSELF

What things do you like to do to help others?
Make a list:

_____

_____

_____

_____

What are other possibilities that you could do to
help others? Make a list:

_____

_____

_____

_____

How important is helping others in your new
    retirement life?

_____

_____

_____

47. Give to those less fortunate

As we all know, life is not fair, and many people
are in poor circumstances through no fault of
their own. Give useful gifts and food to people
who need them. Creative gifts of fruit or new
towels and lovely soap will be much appreciated.
Offer gifts of entertainment with movie passes or
tickets to a special event. Let someone use your
air miles to visit his/her family; your kindness
will never be forgotten.

When is the best time of the day for you to make
your contribution? Is the best time in the early
morning? Could you spare an hour to volunteer
at your neighborhood school to serve breakfast to
children who come to school hungry? This would
be really appreciated by the schools' staffs, that
have in the past few years become burdened with

trying to address all of society's ills manifest in the children, in addition to teaching them to read, write, do arithmetic and become good citizens.

You would find this activity satisfying because you would be making a contribution at the most basic level of life. How can a child concentrate and learn if he is hungry?

Or, is your time of day the late afternoon or evening? What about listening to children read and then reading to them? So many children now have busy working parents who find it difficult to take the time to read to their children. Children learn to love reading by sharing it with someone who cares. They love to learn new words, to talk about what words mean or how else the story might have ended. You might even give them the gift of a dictionary and help them to learn how to use it.

Children learn to read fluently and with expression by reading out loud to others. So, if you can find a young beginning reader and you want to share a wonderful and valuable exp- erience, try reading together. This experience will have life-long benefits for the child and your contribution will never be forgotten.

ASK YOURSELF

What are some useful gifts you can give to those who need them? Make a list:

_____

_____

What are some creative gifts you can give to others? Make a list:

_____

_____

What kind of contribution would you like to make in your new retirement life?

_____

_____

How can you make this happen?

_____

_____

_____

48. Show others the way

So many people do not know how to do specific things and as a result lose so much enjoyment of life. Invite someone in to your home to make bread or cookies with you. Ask someone over to see your workshop and demonstrate how each of the machines works. Volunteer to show someone how to knit, to paint a room, trade online, or to snowshoe. Invite someone to go fishing, hiking or attend church with you. Once people feel familiar in these new surroundings, they will be comfortable going by themselves or with others.

This strategy keeps things simple and produces a win/win situation. You do not need to feel that you must make a continual and energy-draining contribution for it to be worthwhile. So look for something you know would expand the enjoyment of life for others and that you would like to do and make it yours. Enjoy it. Appreciate the improved quality of life you experience and that you bring to others. Your honest, simple contribution will bring virtual meaning to life. You will have discovered a very real purpose for being alive and this will bring you great satisfaction.

Kathleen has always loved music. As a child she took piano lessons and learned to play well enough to bring real pleasure to herself and others. She played for different occasions over the years, helping out with variety shows and annual concerts in her community. As an adult she supported bringing concerts into her hometown so that people, young and old alike, could experience the joy of hearing music performed on stage. In her later years she undertook a major project in raising funds to introduce live musical performances into the school district so that children learn about music early.

Kathleen is passionate about this work and says that it is making a difference in the lives of the children. Some of them are now taking music lessons and a couple of them have even gone to study music at university. They give Kathleen full credit for awakening the love of music within them through the school musical program. A fitting tribute to a woman who makes a great contribution doing something she loves!

ASK YOURSELF

What are some of the things you could show others how to do? Make a list:

_____

_____

_____

_____

How could you make these happen?

_____

_____

_____

_____

What would you gain by showing others the way?

_____

_____

_____

_____

49. Leave reminders for others

Call and remind someone of the lecture you are going to together. Drop the group an email about the lunch you are having. Remind a speaker of the special circumstances of their visit, or let a special person know of their loved one's birthday if you know they sometimes forget. We all want to look good and there are ways to leave reminders that are considerate and timely—and they will be much appreciated.

One of the thoughts in Desiderata is that for all its faults, the world is a beautiful place and it is unfolding as it should. Without the compassionate help of others the world would be a very disheartening place. Just as there is no traditional way to lend a helping hand, our quality of life is diminished if we try to follow others ways of doing things.

ASK YOURSELF

What is something you tend to forget?

_____

_____

_____

Does someone remind you?   Yes/No

What are some things you can do to remind others of things they want to remember? Make a list:

_____

_____

_____

50. Unleash the human spirit

Look for ways to find special meaning in every-thing. There is a purpose to our lives and to the events that make up our lives. We hold a big space of wonder, eternal hope and the belief that things will always be better. There is a big world of gratitude, of giving thanks for all we have, of appreciating the gifts that others bring into our lives. Look for the spirit, the intuitive truth in everything. In this way, you can strengthen your own spiritual core, and your example could inspire the lives of others. One of the most powerful gifts you can give to others is to live your own life full of meaning.

Rosetta was forced to leave her country during a time of terrible civil unrest in the last century. She and some of her sisters fled with the clothes on their backs, grateful to be accepted into our country as refugees. She took domestic work to provide herself with basic food and lodging, and went to night school to learn the English language. Then she wanted to find a way to make a living even though she had very little training.

Rosetta was determined to make a good life for herself. She enrolled in an aesthetician's course and learned to do everything from manicures to massage and electrolysis. She opened her shop in a beauty parlor at first to gain customers and when she had a faithful clientele she moved to her own private little shop.

Over the years, she made a good living and enjoyed caring for her clients. When it was time to retire, Rosetta decided to close her shop several days a week so she could devote this time to people in care homes. She visits regularly and does manicures and pedicures for people. It makes such a difference in their lives, and she has found a place where she can find peace and comfort by being with others. Her contribution is much appreciated and she has a life that is full of meaning.

ASK YOURSELF

What brings special meaning to your life?

_____

_____

_____

_____

What do you believe to be true in this world?

_____

_____

_____

How can you live your life full of meaning? Make
   a list:

_____

_____

_____

How can you inspire the lives of others?

_____

_____

_____

51. Empathize as others reconstruct their lives

Whether it is a friend who has lost a spouse, a neighbor who has had a house fire, or a stranger who needs advice on how to deal with an emergency, trauma affects us all at different times in our lives. Having a clear mind, a steady hand and a kind heart at times like these is wonderfully helpful.

One of my favorite charities is called Dress For Success®. You can find it at www.dressfor success.org. It is an organization that supports women who are returning to the workplace. They receive assistance with their resumes, their interview skills, and mentoring as they re-establish themselves. One practical aspect of this work is that if the woman needs a suit of clothes in which to attend a job interview, she is given a well-fitting, flattering suit to wear. This very practical gesture helps her rebuild her world and sets her off on her new career.

The result is that some of these women return to the organization at a later stage to help and guide others who are in similar situations. They form a professional support group and provide leader-ship and encouragement to other women at a vulnerable time in their lives.

Some people who have been deeply wounded by the events in their lives need help to find peaceful solutions to conflicts in their lives. You can be there with them as they resolve these. Encourage them to apologize, to forgive others, to mourn fully for the injustices of the past. Helping people to reach peaceful solutions allows old wounds to heal and ensures that people bring closure to their past experiences, and leads to them living more authentic and peaceful lives.

ASK YOURSELF

Think of a time when you helped someone construct his or her life. In that experience:

What was present?

_____

_____

_____

_____

How did you get help?

_____

_____

How did you handle trauma?

_____

_____

What qualities do you bring to emergency situations? Make a list:

_____

_____

How can you help others to find peaceful solutions?

_____

_____

52. Strive for peace

At this time in our world, we all need to honor the movement to strive to promote harmony, trust, and healthy relationships. Learn to be peaceful within yourself. Work toward a peaceful community where you live. Model the principles of forgiveness and apology.

"A true culture of peace is based on...principles that promote trust, harmony, and healthy human relationships," says Dr. Louise Diamond in *The Peace Books: 108 simple ways to create a more peaceful world.* Learn more at www.peacebook com.

My personal feeling is that the collective power of women can make a tremendous difference in terms of world peace. While this is not a new idea, and it is spoken about eloquently by the former U.S. secretary of state, Madeline Albright, I realized the potential of this idea this past summer at a family wedding in Eugene, Oregon.

The bride's family has a large number of females who are all well spoken and well educated. As part of the wedding weekend, the women all went out to dinner together. There were over 30 women in the restaurant ranging in age from the early 20's to the late 80's. Each one in turn stood up and talked about love, weddings, the power of love or whatever occurred to them was appropriate for the occasion. I realized that 30 years ago most likely this would not have happened. Not only would the women not have gone out together, at least some of them would have not had the self-esteem and composure to stand up and speak convincingly and with humor. There was real power in that room. It made me realize the tremendous potential for women of all ages, especially retired women with energy and commitment to address collectively the distressing problem of world peace.

ASK YOURSELF

How do you feel about your ability to strive for peace. Do you:

Strive to promote harmony?　　　　　Yes/No
How?

_____

_____

_____

Trust others?   Yes/No
   In what ways?

_____

_____

_____

Promote healthy relationships?   Yes/No
  How?

_____

_____

_____

How else can you work towards peace within
   yourself?

_____

_____

_____

Within your community?

_____

_____

_____

Within the world?

_____

_____

_____

53. Live a life of intention

Decide on the legacy you want to leave in this world. Is it painting? Literature? Teaching? Then live your life so that your actions line up with your intentions. Make each step one of ultimate purpose. Begin as you intend to go forward, and if you are distracted, realign yourself gently and continue on your specially chosen path.

As you proceed, be aware of how privileged you are. You are able to read; you have enough good food and water; you have a comfortable home in which to live. Even more than that, you are free to say what you wish, attend the religious service of your choice, and contact your family members.

People I know have been moved to bring the privileges of our world to others in very intentional ways. One woman has become a lay marriage commissioner. She loves the contact with happy and committed people as they make their marriage vows. Another is a travel companion. She is a life-long learner and keen observer of the cultures and ethnic diversities of the world. She shares these with her travel companions and enriches the lives of them both.

Another woman has become a lay preacher who enjoys sharing her blessings with others. She takes services, and makes home visits to take the blessed sacraments to those who are bed-ridden. She is a blessing herself as she spreads her kindness and her beliefs. And another has learned to be a most inspirational speaker. She brings messages of joy and hope to many organizations, makes new friends, and achieves her purpose of sharing her gratitude for the life she is privileged to lead.

Make your intentions known to family and friends about what you are doing and why you find it so satisfying. Let business clients know how creative you are in the ways you contribute to bettering the world. Write up your experiences and send them out in your Christmas letter and by email to your list of contacts. Challenge others to join you or to compete with you in some way and really get the wheels moving on projects that are important to you. Be willing to take risks outside of your immediate circle of friends and beyond the lines of convention. You will find your circle of influence growing and bringing in so many new ideas, so many new friends and acquaintances into your life that you will virtually enhance the quality of your own life as well as others.

ASK YOURSELF

What do you want to be remembered for?

_____

_____

_____

What do you specifically want to leave behind when you die?

_____

_____

_____

What do you need to do to align your life with your intentions?

_____

_____

_____

How can you let others know what your *new life of intention* will be?

_____

_____

_____

54. Accept your life purpose

Retirement is the time to ask yourself why you were born. It is a time to grow beyond and move to a higher plane. You have had the strength throughout your life to live through the good times and the bad, and now is the time to give up the uninspiring parts of the life you have been living and create the life that is waiting for you.

Larry has always known that his greatest love is nature and he was always happiest at summer camp sharing the beauty of nature through swimming, boating, hiking, and studying nature. When he retired he realized that his life purpose was to share his love of nature with under-privileged children. He set out a plan that allowed him to work with these children throughout the year. These activities included taking the children on outdoor excursions and horse back riding during the school year, and then in the summer months taking them to camp.

This is where he can see his life purpose really come alive! He helps the children collect leaves and stones, he arranges for them to feel the thrill of being in a canoe skimming over the water. They take photographs and then create nature collages throughout the long winter months. Larry lives his love and the children love their experience with nature. Larry has truly moved into the life that was waiting for him.

Now is the time to live your life in alignment with your physical, spiritual and psychological energy. It is the time to walk your talk and create a life that reflects the purpose of your life.

You can now see and understand your life's work. You can give the fullest expression to your spirit as you enjoy the overall manifestation of your personal and spiritual power. You cement your relationship with your divine potential and understand the archetypes that are at work in your life. In all of this, choosing to embrace your life purpose is your greatest power!

ASK YOURSELF

Why do you think you were born? For what purpose?

_____

_____

_____

How are you currently living your life purpose?

_____

_____

_____

Who else do you need to be in your retirement life
to accept your life purpose?

_____

_____

55. Live your mission

How would you describe your life? Is it a rainbow
full of colors that arches over the landscape? Is it
like a shooting star that arcs across the sky filling
people with wonder? Find the analogy or the
image for your life mission. Write it down. "I am
a.... that..." "I am Mother Nature who embodies
my own and others' personal power."

Make it yours. Work it into your personal logo!
Paint it and print it and make stickers with it!

Repeat your mission statement to yourself every day. Reach out to others as you manifest this mission in your life. You will feel fulfilled and powerful and others will see and feel your influence. It is the ultimate in empowering your life and leading a fulfilling life in retirement.

So honor your self in all its glory, all its imagination, and all its belief in the fact that we change the world one day at a time, one person at a time. Your new confidence will bring great satisfaction into your life and you will know that you have done your very best! What could be better than that?

ASK YOURSELF

Which metaphor fits your life? Is it:

A rainbow?   Yes/No

A shooting star?   Yes/No

A river?   Yes/No

If yes, how does it work?

_____

_____

_____

If no, what analogy does work for your life?

_____

_____

_____

How can you make the analogy of your life mission come alive? Make a list:

_____

_____

_____

AFTERWORD

I want to wish you every success in Creating Your Retirement!

Each one of you has a unique personality with special talents, personal dreams and cherished hopes. By following the 55 valuable ways to empower the rest of your life, you can make retirement the most fulfilling time of your life. I hope that you will do that!

Send me your thoughts, ideas and stories of what is special in your retirement life. I will be waiting to hear from you.

Good luck and remember—
For all the sad words of tongue or pen
the saddest are these, *"It might have been!"*

John Greenleaf Whittier from *Maud Muller*   *BMW*

Barbara M. Walker can be reached at:
    Barbara M. Walker Inc.
    Retirement Lifestyle Coach
    Email: barbara@bmwalker.com
    Web: www.bmwalker.com

Resources

As you create your fulfilling retirement lifestyle, most of the resources you need are within yourself. Throughout *Create Your Retirement*®, I have encouraged you to look at your own strengths, skills, talents and dreams to create your own unique, fulfilling life.

There are thousands of resources available for your consideration at your local library and on the Internet. You will find a list of government and community sources worldwide at www.lib.umich.edu/govdocs/webdirec.html.

Organizations specific to retirees are also plentiful. Begin with The National Council on Aging, Inc. at www.ncoa.org.

Books I found useful include:

Books

Alboher, Marci. *the encore handbook: how to make a living and a difference in the second half of life.* Introduction by Marc Freedman, Founder and CEO of Encore.org. Civic Ventures, 2013.

Anthony, Mitch. *The New Retirementality: Planning Your Life and Living Your Dream at Any Age You Want.* Dearborn Financial Publishing, Inc., 2001.

Bridges, William. *Making Sense of Life's Transitions.* Addison-Wesley, 1980.

Burgett, Gordon. *How to Create Your Own Super Second Life: What are you going to do with your extra 30 years?* *Communications Unlimited, Santa Maria,* California, 1999.

Cimoroni, Sandy, Beth Grudzinski and Patricia Lovett-Reid. *Retirement Strategies for Women.* Key Porter Books Ltd., 1997.

Eisenberg, Lee. *The Number: A Completely Different Way to Think About the Rest of Your Life.* FreePress, 2006.

Fortgang, Laura Berman. *Take Yourself to the Top.* New York, Warner Books, 1998.

Fettke, Rich. *Extreme Success: The 7-Part Program That Shows You How to Succeed Without Struggle.* New York, Fireside/Simon & Schuster, 2002.

Frankl, Victor. *Man's Search For Meaning. Pocket Books, 1959.*

Freedman, Marc. *encore: finding work that matters in the second half of life.* PublicAffairs, 2007.

Hay, Louise. *You Can Heal Your Life.* Hay House, Carson, CA., 1984.

Jamal, Azim and Harvey McKinnon. *The Power of Giving: Creating Abundance in your home, at work, and in your community.* Tides Canada Foundation, 2005.

Jeffers, Susan. *Feel the Fear and Do It Anyway.* New York, Ballantine Books, 1987.

Johnson, Richard P. Ph.D. *what color is your retirement? The LifeOptions guidebook to discover, plan and live your retirement dream.* Retirement Options, St. Louis, Missouri, 2006.

Kelley, Rob. *The Complete Guide to a Creative Retirement.* Turnkey Press, 2003.

Landy, Samantha. *Savvy Senior Singles: Navigating the Singles World From 50 and Beyond.* Destiny Image Publishers, Inc., 2007.

McNally, David. *Even Eagles Need a Push.* Dell Publishing, 1990.

Miedaner, Talane. *Coach Yourself To Success.* Contemporary Books, 2000.

Pierce, Penney. *The Intuitive Way: A Guide to Living from Inner Wisdom.* Beyond Words Publishing, Inc., 1997.

Rich, Phil, Dorothy Madway Sampson and Dale S. Fetherling. *The Healing Journey Through Retirement.* John Wiley & Sons, Inc., 2000.

Roadburg, Dr. Alan. *What Are You Doing After Work? A Retirement Lifestyle Planning Guide.* AGF Management, Ltd., 2002.

Sadler, William A. Ph.D. *The Third Age: 6 Principles for Growth and Renewal After Forty.* Da Capo Press, 2000.

Schlossberg, Nancy K. Ed.D. *Retire Smart, Retire Happy: Finding Your True Path in Life.* APA Life Tools, 2004. Alpha Books, 2007.

Sedlar, Jeri and Rick Miners. *Don't Retire, Rewire!* Second edition, Alpha books, Penguin Group, 2007.

Sher, Barbara, and Gottlieb, Annie. *Wishcraft.* New York: The Viking Press, 1979.

_____, and Barbara Smith. *I Could Do Anything If I Only Knew What It Was.* New York: Delecorte Press, 1994.

St. John, Noah. *Learn How and Why to Give Yourself Permission to Succeed.* Health Communications. Inc., 1999.

Stone, Marika and Howard. *Too Young to Retire: 101 Ways to Start the Rest of Your Life.* Penguin, 2002.

Trafford, Abigail. *My Time: Making the Most of the Rest of Your Life.* Basic Books, 2004.